T0389436

Playing with Teaching

Gaming Ecologies and Pedagogies Series

Series Editors

VOLUME 4

The titles published in this series are listed at *brill.com/geps*

Playing with Teaching

Considerations for Implementing Gaming Literacies in the Classroom

Edited by

Antero Garcia, Shelbie Witte and Jennifer S. Dail

BRILL
SENSE

LEIDEN | BOSTON

All chapters in this book have undergone peer review.

The Library of Congress Cataloging-in-Publication Data is available online at http://catalog.loc.gov

Typeface for the Latin, Greek, and Cyrillic scripts: "Brill". See and download: brill.com/brill-typeface.

ISSN 2589-9880
ISBN 978-90-04-42230-8 (paperback)
ISBN 978-90-04-38874-1 (hardback)
ISBN 978-90-04-42231-5 (e-book)

This book is printed on acid-free paper and produced in a sustainable manner.

Contents

Foreword

You're a teacher. Maybe you are a gamer. Then again, maybe you are not.

I am a teacher, but I am not a gamer. Then again, I remember as a child and an adolescent enjoying checkers, chess, *Monopoly*, *Trouble*, and a few others. I've also spent hours as an adult playing *Trivial Pursuit*, *Apples to Apples*, and *Settlers of Catan*. Now that I think about it, I also play *Texas Hold 'Em* once in a while with friends. And, I like *Blackjack* now and then when I'm on vacation. And, I was pretty big into *Dungeons & Dragons* when I was in high school. I also loved Choose-Your-Own-Adventure novels, which made reading a book from beginning to end an old-fashioned activity.

I am not a gamer. Then again, I remember how excited we kids were when we got *Pong* in the early 1970s, literally leaping in the air with glee when our grandparents brought it for Christmas. Who knew how exciting it could be to watch a small square of light move slowly from a rectangle of light ("thunk") to another rectangle of light ("thunk") and back? Atari arrived some years later with *Space Invaders* and *Asteroids*, which meant I could play without begging for quarters. The game *Adventure* taught me about Easter eggs, and *Dragon's Lair* brought full animation and narrative to games. Later, I spent hours exploring the world of *Myst*, solving puzzles and reading secret volumes in an ever-evolving story with a book-slamming ending.

I am not a gamer. But then again, I meet with a financial manager once a year to plan for retirement, during which time we predict how the stock market will perform the following year. My very livelihood if I retire depends on how well I play the market.

I am not a gamer. But then again, I know that as Wittgenstein has taught us, much of oral communication can be described accurately as "language games", which include turn taking, rule following, insider knowledge, and rhetorical strategy. As interlocutors, we compose new conversations with new players and new rules all the time.

I am not a gamer. But then again, I have participated in romantic and platonic relationships, some replete with what the British band Foreigner dubbed "Head Games". Even in a quarter-century-old marriage, I play games. For example, The Making My Wife Laugh game, for which, sadly, laughs only count when I get them for something I do on purpose. Or the more strenuous How Can I Not Do the Dishes Tonight game.

I'm not a gamer. But then again, I was a dean for a few years, and I recall the power games I had to contend with. Emails became flaming swords with plus or minus points for charisma and experience. Collecting coins became more literal each semester, and at some point, I ran out of lives.

I am not a gamer. Then again, I send writing to different journals and publishers, each of which has a different set of rules and processes. Playing well doesn't guarantee a publication, but playing poorly guarantees rejection. Getting enough publications can lead to bonuses at work, even leveling up (promotion), which increases one's voting power and unlocks more choice of classes, and other quests.

I am not a gamer. Then again, I remember learning (and for a while teaching) the five-paragraph essay as a way to outsmart any standardized writing assignment. Use the essay prompt as the first sentence of the essay and make a simple thesis statement. Make three points with two reasons each. Restate the thesis at the end. This formula will work to pass any standardized exam. And will also game the system, rendering its results basically useless as an assessment of writing. As a teacher, I conducted way too many mock *Jeopardy!* tournaments to assess and review low-level knowledge (trivia) from my students.

When I started reading *Playing with Teaching: Considerations for Implementing Gaming Literacies in the Classroom,* I did not think of myself as a gamer. But as I read, I realized I may be a gamer after all. Maybe this is something I should take a bit more seriously as a teacher.

Much in our real lives can be considered a game, a first-person-perspective role play in which we apply knowledge and experience to make choices and then cope with the consequences of those actions. We learn from those adventures and better prepare ourselves for the next set of challenges.

If games are such powerful parts of our lives, "Why not apply that same level of real-world thought and adventure to English classes?" Garcia, Dail, and Witte's book asks us. Great question!

Antero Garcia, Shelbie Witte, and Jennifer S. Dail have gathered a collection of essays that do several important things for us teachers:

- They remind us of the joy that really good games can elicit.
- They help us understand the innovative, rule-bound creativity involved in genuine critical thinking.
- They demonstrate for us ways to use games and gameful design to create classrooms that are more authentic, more rigorous, and more engaging than traditional instruction is or can be.

Drawing on English education, cognitive science, educational psychology, linguistics, game design, literary analysis, and other fields, the authors in *Playing with Teaching* make a compelling case for bringing a more serious form of gaming into ELA classes. Even better, they demonstrate options for successful implementation and explore how high-level critical-thinking games work in real classroom situations.

Summer campers come together and build their own games, some from stacks of pipe-cleaners, play money, and rubber animals, and others from software designed for game builders. In so doing, the young people learn how to design rules, regulate rigor, and vary activity to inspire genuine engagement in critical thinking, all with guidance from their National Writing Project-educated counselors.

Narrative-based games – and there are many – immerse young people in worlds of words, asking them to empathize with different kinds of people with different kinds of challenges. We can explore those narratives for how they define our world – even how they define the very concept of youth (as one chapter does). We can place narratives in games against narratives in novels, exploring their contrasts (as another chapter does). We can ask students to incorporate stories into their own games or use them to explore their own perspectives. We teachers can ensure that our incorporation of technology in games (and otherwise) aligns effectively with appropriate pedagogical content knowledge, as yet another chapter explores.

Teachers who are open to new ways of teaching, who want to ensure their students are doing a lot of thinking in their classes will appreciate this book's approaches. There are games for low-tech and high-tech teachers. There are multi-player and single-player games that teachers can employ to help students with collaborative or more solitary literacies. There are ways to engage students in talk about games that don't even require playing games in the classroom.

Readers will also find references to an amount of research on games and literacy that may surprise them. Thinking of learning as play is nothing new, but literal game play has become so ubiquitous and so absorbing for so many young people, it behooves us to think about it from a professional standpoint and to incorporate it more directly into our classes.

Playing games is serious work. But all work and no play makes us all very dull people. Gaming, gameful design, and gamification in and of English Language Arts classes can ensure that teachers and students are at work and at play at the same time.

Whether readers just check in or go all in, Garcia, Witte and Dail's collection will inspire creative thinking and new ways of engaging students in the enduring skills and knowledge of literacy. Can you come out and play?

Ken Lindblom
Professor of English
Stony Brook University

Figures and Tables

Figures

Tables

Notes on Contributors

Jill Bindewald
taught English in middle and high school for ten years. Now she is a Ph.D. student at Oklahoma State University in the Literacy, Language, and Culture program in which she focuses on Place-Conscious Education and Rural Literacies.

Jennifer S. Dail
is a Professor of English education in the Department of English at Kennesaw State University in the metro-Atlanta area of Georgia. She also directs the Kennesaw Mountain Writing Project (KMWP), a National Writing Project site serving teachers Pre-K through college in all content areas. Dail served as coeditor of *SIGNAL Journal*, the International Literacy Association's journal focusing on young adult literature, from 2008 to 2013. She is also an active member of several educational organizations including the National Council of Teachers of English (NCTE) and the National Writing Project (NWP). She serves on the board of the Georgia Council of Teachers of English (GCTE) as the First Vice President and Conference Director. Dail has published multiple articles on young adult literature and technology in *The ALAN Review* and has written book chapters focusing on this work as well. She also co-edited *Toward a More Visual Literacy: Shifting the Paradigm with Digital Tools and Young Adult Literature* (Rowman and Littlefield, 2018) and *Young Adult Literature and the Digital World: Textual Engagement through Visual Literacy* (Rowman and Littlefield, 2018), both with Shelbie Witte and Steven Bickmore.

Elizabeth DeBoeser
is an English Language Arts teacher at H.J. MacDonald Middle School in New Bern, North Carolina. She earned her Master's of Arts in Education at the College of William & Mary. During her time there, she became interested in how tabletop role-playing games can inform and enrich English Language Arts instruction.

Antero Garcia
is an Assistant Professor in the Graduate School of Education at Stanford University where he studies how technology and gaming shape both youth and adult learning, literacy practices, and civic identities. Prior to completing his Ph.D., Antero was an English teacher at a public high school in South Central Los Angeles. His most recent research studies explore learning and literacies in tabletop roleplaying games *Dungeons & Dragons* and how participatory culture shifts classroom relationships and instruction. Based on his research focused

on equitable teaching and learning opportunities for urban youth through the use of participatory media and gameplay, Antero co-designed the Critical Design and Gaming School – a public high school in South Central Los Angeles. Antero's research has appeared in numerous journals including *The Harvard Educational Review, Teachers College Record,* and *Reading and Writing Quarterly.* His most recent books are *Good Reception: Teens, Teachers, and Mobile Media in a Los Angeles High School, Doing Youth Participatory Action Research: Transforming Inquiry with Researchers, Educators, and Students* (with Nicole Mirra and Ernest Morrell; MIT Press, 2017), and *Pose, Wobble, Flow: A Culturally Proactive Approach to Literacy Instruction* (with Cindy O'Donnell-Allen; Teachers College Press, 2015). Antero received his Ph.D. in the Urban Schooling division of the Graduate School of Education and Information Studies at the University of California, Los Angeles.

Kip Glazer
is an experienced classroom educator who won the Kern County Teacher of the Year in 2014. In 2015, she received her doctorate in Learning Technologies from Pepperdine University for her research on game-based learning. She was named the Principal at San Marcos High School in Santa Barbara in March 2019.

Emily Howell
is a faculty member in literacy for Clemson University's College of Education in the Department of Education and Human Development. Emily has taught English and writing at the secondary and collegiate level and currently teaches pre-service teachers and graduate students in education, employing both online and face-to-face classroom environments. Her research interests include multiliteracies, adolescent literacy, writing instruction, and digital tools. Her research has been published in journals such as *Journal of Literacy Research, The Reading Teacher, Journal of Adolescent and Adult Literacy,* and *Professional Development in Education.*

Lindy L. Johnson
is Assistant Professor of English Education at College of William & Mary. Prior to pursuing her Ph.D. in Language and Literacy from The University of Georgia, she taught high school English in Boston Public Schools. Her research draws on sociocultural theories of mediated action to examine the kinds of instructional supports both teachers and adolescents find helpful in comprehending and creating complex multimodal texts.

Rachel Kaminski Sanders
received her doctoral degree from The University of Georgia after producing a text-free dissertation. Rachel seeks to broaden the types of scholarly research compositions traditionally accepted within higher education, an area she feels is imperative to advancing academic research. Prior to her doctoral program, Rachel taught seventh grade writing at a public arts magnet school in a rural district located in the state of South Carolina. Rachel is currently an Assistant Professor of Literacy Education in the Department of Interdisciplinary Learning and Teaching at The University of Texas at San Antonio.

Ken Lindblom
teaches graduate and undergraduate courses in pedagogy, literature, and non-fiction, at Stony Brook University. He is a former Dean in the School of Professional Development (2014-2018), and he directed the English Teacher Education Program at Stony Brook from 2003-2016. He is co-author of the *Continuing the Journey* book series with Leila Christenbury (National Council of Teachers of English, 2017).

Jon Ostenson
first encountered the storytelling power of video games in the 1980s, thanks to interactive fiction titles like *Adventure* and *Zork*. Today, he is Associate Professor of English Education at Brigham Young University. A former high school English teacher, he has long sought to bring into the classroom the texts teenagers read and interact with outside the classroom.

Chad Sansing
is the Practice Lead for Open Culture & Curriculum at the Mozilla Foundation. He is passionate about helping people design and build projects and cultures that empower people to collaborate within inclusive communities. In a past life, he taught middle school for 14 years and worked to democratize the public school classroom.

Shelbie Witte
is the Chuck and Kim Watson Endowed Chair in Education and Professor in Adolescent Literacy and English Education at Oklahoma State University, where she directs the OSU Writing Project and the Initiative for 21st Century Literacies Research. She serves as editor (with Sara Kajder) of *Voices from the Middle*, NCTE's premiere middle-level journal. Witte has published extensively in the area of 21st Century Literacies, including *Literacy Engagement through*

Peritextual Analysis (American Library Association and National Council of Teachers of English, 2019) with Don Latham and Melissa Gross, *Toward a More Visual Literacy: Shifting the Paradigm with Digital Tools and Young Adult Literature* (Rowman & Littlefield, 2018) and *Young Adult Literature and the Digital World: Textual Engagement Through Visual Literacy* (Rowman and Littlefield, 2018), both with Jennifer S. Dail and Steven Bickmore.

INTRODUCTION

Taking Literacies of Play Seriously

Antero Garcia, Jennifer S. Dail and Shelbie Witte

Describing some of the most memorable aspects of playing a videogame like the narrative driven *Firewatch*, videogame YouTube channel Satchbag's Goods (2016) notes that some of the feelings of fulfilling come "in the conversations had after the game is done, they thrive on the viscerally grey *in* the world and *outside* of it". As a game in which you navigate and unravel mysteries within the game and also reflect upon and make further empathetic connections "outside" the game, *Firewatch* is not a wholly unique game in this regard. Instead, Satchbag's Goods emphasizes some of the key possibilities of literacies, learning, and play. Not only can a game like *Firewatch* support powerful in-game literacy practices – reading, writing upon, and mediating interactions within the world of the game, but it can also foster "real" world relationships and function as a text on which individuals can ascribe meaning, remix, and build connections to other ideas, identities, and epistemologies. Play – as a critical, and literacy-rich act – *is* learning.

This volume interrogates the relationships and possibilities between literacies, pedagogies, and play. Each of the contributors to this book shares insights from within digital and non-digital playful contexts and offers powerful ideas for transforming pedagogy and learning. However, before we dig more deeply into the learning opportunities we imagine can be developed and sustained in classrooms, we want to briefly detour and look at organic learning and play in out-of-school settings.

1 Assembling Playful Learning Opportunities

> There is a box of plastic animals, insects, and dinosaurs that are all dumped onto the table where players take turns selecting their beasts. As you might in the wild, they typically go for the larger predators first. Once they have selected and arranged their beasts opposite each other, the battling beings. One person puts forth an animal (or several animals), and the other person counters with an opponent (or opponents), and we call out how many 6-sided dice we think each one is worth. We usually agree on the strength of an animal, but sometimes [my son] comes in a

 | DOI: 10.1163/9789004422315_001

> little high, in which case we compromise. For instance, a wolf has a score range of 4–24 with four six-sided die, but a range of 1–24 with the d24 … so more opportunity for an upset. This aspect to the game has been interesting for my son, especially when he rolls a 2 with that big d30 and a tiger loses to a fly rolling a d4. This idea of chance – of no guarantee even when a win is heavily favored – seems pretty crucial to the idea of a good game. (D. Crovitz, personal communication, April 24, 2017)

Jennifer was at her friend Darren's house watching him and his young son play a game that they had imagined and created together. As a game that cannot be formally purchased in a store – and one that would likely lose its homegrown charm if so – we want to highlight the complex *systems* that are constructed, understood, and interacted with upon the table. This was something that a young child and parent created together. Their mutually constituted system of rules was defined through the interests and whims of the participants (e.g. Gallego, Cole, & Laboratory of Comparative Human Cognition, 2001; Pacheco & Gutiérrez, 2009). These rules and systems are an important distinction for types of play and games as we explore in this book. Specifically, constraints in this example and more generally fuel imagination and mediate forms of interaction, co-learning, and identity development. From what kinds of choices individuals can make within the game to the role that materials play, systems foster – rather than hinder – the bevvy of literacy practices afforded to players. Artifacts – dice, plastic animals – as well as a space in which to interact are crucial to understanding play as well. In this sense, *space* matters when considering the literacy and learning of participants (e.g. Leander & Sheehy, 2004; Massey, 2005). Though Darren and his son's game takes place in an environment that looks very different from and functions away from the traditional constraints of most classrooms, we highlight it as a robust context to guide our conceptions of power, pedagogy, literacies, and learning.

2 Games are Purpose-Driven

Returning to classroom learning, the kinds of practices that Darren and his son engage in are not hard to foster in schools. Gaming can help adolescents feel purposeful – that they have meaningful contributions to make to the world in which they live. In Nathan Hill's (2016) novel *The Nix*, Pwnage, a gamer, meets Samuel, another online player, in real life. In this meeting, Pwnage claims that the work he does in the novel's game *Elfscape* is more meaningful than what he does in the real world. In *Elfscape* he is a leader who brings players together to leverage their strengths and assets to kill creatures and level up, where no single player could accomplish this alone. Pwnage explains, "Listen, what I do in *Elfscape* matters. Like, the things I do affect the larger system. They change the world. You cannot say this about real life" (p. 191). He continues by claiming, "We're fulfilling our basic human psychological need to feel meaningful and significant" (p. 192). We want to emphasize that the work, the relationships, and the learning that happens in gaming environments *do* matter. We agree that - for many of our students, these *are* spaces that are more meaningful and more "real" than *real* life. Arguably these connections to other people, to specific goals, and to purposeful production are what adolescents seek, and these are things gaming affords them.

It is all too easy to assume that when youth are not performing well within school-based frameworks that they are disengaged with literacy practices. In reality what they are more likely disengaged with is school itself. Adolescents seek out their own spaces where they participate in activities that hold high interest for them. These activities could range from, but are certainly not limited to, reading young adult novels to gaming. Gee (2004) argues that adolescents carve out and actively participate in passion-driven "affinity spaces". Gaming offers one such space that leverages the features Gee outlines as defining characteristics of affinity spaces. In short, participants in these spaces generate and share knowledge, participate through a variety of routes, gain status, and flex in and out of leadership roles within the space.

In an interview reflecting on games, literacies, and learning (Mora et al., 2020) discussed the role of perspective, advances in how we understand learning practices, and the possible futures of play and learning. Considering how to better systematically engage in the robust learning practices within games, Mora asks, "What can we do to help take literacies of play seriously?" Gee's response calls for "explicating play in terms of what are the identities we use, what are the skills we use, [and] what are the norms we use" (Mora et al., 2020). Gee goes on to consider how "the literacies of play" include "your knowledge of the values, skills, norms, activity, practices, and ways of being in the world of a gamer" (Mora et al., 2020). These are complex, layered practices and identities. What it means to *be* a gamer varies from context to context, culture to culture. And yet, each environment is one that carries with it particular, unique learning affordances. Echoing Pwnage's assertion, what happens in games and playful learning environments "matters".

As we consider the affordances of play – whether it is at a table with improvised rules and toys or within the digitally robust virtual world of *Firewatch* – we want to recognize that the contexts of playing and learning today are substantively different than generations past. On devices in their pockets, laptops in their backpacks, dice and boards on countertops, and complex, web-enabled consoles in their living rooms, games are a big deal for young people today. Nearly all other forms of capitalist entertainment are dwarfed by the booming $99.6 billion video game industry (Minnoti, 2016). More than simply products for consumption, games today serve as a rich foundation for participatory youth to engage in various fandoms, build complex relationships, and become media-savvy, multimodal producers in their own right. Games are weaving a tapestry of interest-driven "connected learning" for young people (Ito et al., 2013).

By exploring how youth are authentically engaging in literacy practices in games and gaming communities, the authors in this book share specific strategies for educators to bring gaming into their classrooms. The authors in this book explore ways adolescents read and engage with the world around them to construct meaning and to examine how teachers can leverage these practices within their own classrooms. The theoretical framework of *playful pedagogical content knowledge* (described in the next section) is illustrated by practical examples, which are currently absent from the conversation. Finally, the authors in this book examine how teachers and caring mentors guide adolescents' in implementing digital literacies to create remixes and mashups, engage in participatory cultures, participate in transmedia experiences, and exercise multimodalities.

Considering the complex demands in public schools today and the niche pockets of extracurricular engagement in which youth find themselves, this book serves as a hands-on resource for teachers and teacher educators. Particularly focused on how games – both digital and non-digital – can shape unique learning and literacy experiences for young people today, this book's chapters look at specific examples that educators can bring into their classrooms today.

3 Looking Ahead: Toward Playful Pedagogical Content Knowledge

Foundational in describing the skills of teachers, Lee Shulman (1986) notes that *pedagogical content knowledge* "goes beyond knowledge of subject matter per se to the dimension of subject matter knowledge for teaching" (p. 9). Within domains like math, science, or English, such knowledge includes ways of conveying complex information, tailoring instruction to a particular set of students, and learning what lessons may be difficult. At its heart, pedagogical content knowledge can be understood as "preparing lessons that are designed around "the conceptions and preconceptions that students of different ages and backgrounds bring with them to the learning of those most frequently taught topics and lessons" (p. 9).

As we are optimistic about helping further the deliberate integration of gaming in classrooms, we wonder what a *playful* pedagogical content knowledge might look like? What does it mean to consider the conversation *around* a game like *Firewatch* or to improvise complex gaming systems like Darren does for his son? What does it mean to re-think curriculum in ways that it is seen as playful constraints and gameful opportunities for personal growth (e.g. McGonigal, 2015)? Across the chapters in this volume, kernels of playful pedagogical content knowledge emerge and we are hopeful for the collective inquiry we can all playfully engage in.

This book functions as a standalone title tied to a forthcoming Brill Sense title by the same editors – *Studying Gaming Literacies: Theories to Inform Classroom Practice* (2020). Focused specifically on the narratives of games and learning in classroom settings, the book you are holding builds on games and learning research to illustrate how teachers can leverage play within schools. With each chapter offering specific pedagogical strategies and connections to research, this volume seeks to fill a much-needed space in how games are applied in classrooms today.

By exploring how teachers can support literacy practices through gaming, this book shares specific strategies for heightening the experiences of students. Aligned to the theoretical framework reinforced in our companion volume, we offer several practical examples of games and learning, which are currently absent from the conversation. This book seeks to examine how teachers and mentors can guide adolescents' take-up of digital literacies to create remixes and mashups, engage in participatory cultures, participate in transmedia experiences, and exercise multimodalities.

Considering the complex demands in public schools today and the niche pockets of extracurricular engagement in which youth find themselves, this book serves as a hands-on resource for teachers and teacher educators today. Providing specific examples and theories for educators to play with in classrooms today, this volume does not presume to offer a panacea to the legacies of historical inequities in schools today. Instead, we see this as a platform for playful collaboration that intentionally seeks to upend existing systems of inequitable opportunities with resources for democratic, transformative play.

References

Gallego, M. A., Cole, M., & Laboratory of Comparative Human Cognition. (2001). Classroom culture and culture in the classroom. In V. Richardson (Ed.), *Handbook of research on teaching* (4th ed., pp. 951–997). Washington, DC: American Educational Research Association.

Gee, J. P. (2004). *Situated language and learning: A critique of traditional schooling.* New York, NY: Routledge.

Ito, M., Gutierrez, K., Livingstone, S., Penuel, B., Rhodes, J., Salen, K., et al. (2013). *Connected learning: An agenda for research and design.* Irvine, CA: Digital Media and Learning Research Hub.

Leander, K. M., & Sheehy, M. (Eds.). (2004). *Spatializing literacy research and practice.* New York, NY: Peter Lang.

Massey, D. (2005). *For space.* London: Sage.

McGonigal, J. (2015). *Super better: A revolutionary approach to getting stronger, happier, braver and more resilient.* New York, NY: Penguin.

Minotti, M. (2016). Video games will become a $99.6B industry this year as mobile overtakes consoles and PCs. *Venture Beat.* Retrieved from https://venturebeat.com/2016/04/21/video-games-will-become-a-99-6b-industry-this-year-as-mobile-overtakes-consoles-and-pcs/

Mora, R. A., Gee, J. P., Hernandez, M., Castaño, Orrego, T. S., & Ramírez, D. (2020). Literacies of play: Blazing the trail, unchartered territories, and hurrying up – #Teamlav's interview with James Paul Gee. In A. Garcia, S. Witte, & J. Dail (Eds.), *Studying gaming literacies: Theories to inform classroom practice.* Leiden, The Netherlands (forthcoming): Brill Sense.

Pacheco, M., & Gutiérrez, K. (2008). Cultural-historical approaches to literacy, teaching and learning. In C. Compton-Lilly (Ed.), *Breaking the silence: Recognizing the social and cultural resources students bring to the classroom* (pp. 60–77). Newark, DE: International Reading Association.

Satchbag's Goods. (2016). *Firewatch is mine.* Retrieved from https://www.youtube.com/watch?v=Z74nUBkMdSg

Shulman, L. S. (1986). Those who understand: Knowledge growth in teaching. *Educational Researcher, 15*(2), 4–14.

PART 1

Writing and Text-Based Models of Play

Introduction to Part 1: Writing and Text-Based Models of Play

Antero Garcia, Shelbie Witte and Jennifer S. Dail

We begin this volume with four chapters focusing on production, writing, and how young people are engaged in specific kinds of learning content and concepts. As we look at what students make, what tools they utilized in their authorship, and the kinds of learning that students demonstrated, it is important to note what aspects of teaching and writing are foregrounded and what is less visible. Some of these differences are a matter of vocabulary – prewriting and revising, for example, are often seen as prototyping and playtesting. Likewise, assessment can be viewed differently through games and their creation. On the one hand, a cynical view is that these chapters downplay the role of assessing learning – students make what they want, how they want, and run amok within digital and analog play-based learning environments. However, more realistically, the completed games and the experiences they sustain are the assessment. Gee's (2007) scholarship has emphasized that playing a videogame is its own kind of formative assessment; when you beat a difficult game that task is demonstrative of a kind of proficiency. Similarly, finishing making a game represents a mastery of some skill sets; these can be clearly signaled in the design constraints and challenges when making games.

In addition to foregrounding particular aspects of instruction and learning, we see these chapters as highlighting kinds of tools and practices for making games. Though Howell & Sanders and Sanders (in a separate, single-authored analysis) illustrate some key resources for videogame design – Gamestar Mechanic and Scratch are programs that many educators we have worked with have adapted smoothly into classrooms – the principles for game design are tool-agnostic. Instead, all of these chapters underscore the importance of imagination, collaboration, and design-based thinking. If materials and technologies have seemed like a barrier to leveraging a gameful pedagogy in classrooms, these chapters challenge such assumptions. Further, across all of these chapters, we draw your attention to the practical elements that are shared. Howell and Sanders share weekly and daily schedules to highlight what their moment-to-moment and day-to-day instruction looked like. Likewise Johnson and DeBoeser offer clear step by step directions for how they supported the creation and playing of tabletop roleplaying games in classrooms.

 | DOI: 10.1163/9789004422315_002

While there are a smattering of tools and practices in these chapters that teachers can adapt, more importantly are the recurring themes heard across these contributions. In an interview conducted by Oklahoma State University pre-service teachers with the designers and founders of Thorny Games, Kathryn Hymes and Hakan Seyaliogolu, emphasize that story and empathy are the most important parts of making games. This reflects what Johnson and DeBoeser stressed, even as they were working through complex connections between novels and forms of play.

At the heart of a good story and empathy are the possibilities of play. As Hymes reflects on her role as a designer, play – as an important component of how people interact and learn – is a fundamental core of what to preserve in what individuals make and interact with:

> I think another part of what we do, and it really is about trying to put something good into the world, is actually spreading play just for the sake of play. There's so much value in being playful as adults. We are encultured to stop doing that at a certain age, and I feel like that's a very confining negative thing for a healthy well-rounded and optimistic life. You see baby animals, baby humans ... Play just naturally bursts from them and it's only through these societal pressures and structures that adults stop doing it. Just spreading the value and preaching play is another element of what we make.

Neither these contributors nor we as this volume's editors believe that there is a silver-bullet solution to supporting games and learning in schools. However, looking beyond the right tools and focusing instruction on play, empathy, and story feel like necessary steps forward for all teachers. Such instruction is not only transformative for students and teachers but it is also – importantly – fun.

Reference

Gee, J. P. (2007). *What video games have to teach us about learning and literacy* (Rev. and updated ed). New York, NY: Palgrave Macmillan.

CHAPTER 1

Writing through Gaming: A Youth Writing Camp Perspective

Emily Howell and Rachel Kaminski Sanders

1 Overarching Questions

1. In what ways can outside of school spaces challenge conventional notions of reading and literacy instruction?
2. How can gaming practices strengthen literacy practices?
3. What stakeholders are positioned to assist educators with expanding instructional practices outside of schools?

2 Introduction

In this chapter we discuss how a gaming camp combined writing and gaming, both literacy practices. Through activities such as quick writes, games design, and collaboratively sharing and publishing this design, we address how teachers might integrate in a practical manner what have remained largely theoretical concepts, such as multimodality, social practice, and participatory culture. We examine instructional practices that might develop and challenge the conventional concept of writing in the field of English/language arts (ELA) and how they were enacted in a summer youth camp for gaming organized by a National Writing Project (NWP) site.[1]

3 Statement of the Problem

Reading, writing, the narrative, and visual literacy all seem inherent to gaming, but they are not easily separable, which is representative of the indistinct parameters inherent in the digital age, as opposed to more conventional literacy skills (Alberti, 2008). Perhaps due to this fluid nature of conventional and digital literacies involved in gaming, more research is needed on how it might be integrated into literacy classrooms, in which teachers value technology, but struggle to integrate it effectively (Hutchison & Reinking, 2011;

 | DOI: 10.1163/9789004422315_003

Peterson & McClay, 2012). The importance of how technology is integrated, especially whether it is used in passive or participatory practices, is highlighted in research focusing on the effectiveness of technology for learning being tied to its use in the classroom (Carter, Greenberg, & Walker, 2016; Means & Peters, 2016). Although gaming may entail practices laudable in learning and discussed in the last decade via theoretical perspectives such as Henry Jenkins and colleagues' (Jenkins, Clinton, Purushotma, Robison, & Weigel, 2006; Jenkins, Ito, & boyd, 2015) participatory cultures and James Gee's learning principles from gaming (Gee, 2007), many adults remain divided about how they view gaming.

For instance, a Pew Internet study (Duggan, 2015) found that a similar percentage of adults think games are a waste of time (26%) as do those who do not think this is true (24%). Similarly, 17% of adults think games help develop problem solving and strategy thinking, but 16% think this is not true. There are mixed opinions regarding the value of gaming in the adult population as a whole. Perhaps surprisingly, teachers may be more open to gaming and its potential learning benefits (Takeuchi & Vaala, 2014).

4 Relevant Literature and Perspectives

4.1 *Gaming and Teaching*

Takeuchi and Vaala (2014) conducted a survey of 694 K-8 practicing teachers and found that 74% of teachers report using games for instruction. However, those using games were younger teachers, who were game players themselves. In addition, these teachers needed more guidance in integrating games in instruction. For instance, 80% of teachers using these games wished it was easier to find games aligned with instruction and for both teachers who played games and those who did not, being unsure of how to integrate games into instruction was a high-ranking barrier. Furthermore, Takeuchi and Vaala (2014) saw a need for teachers to use games beyond "drill-and-practice" (p. 6) implementation and called for alternative means for integrating gaming into curriculum. Examining how gaming may be integrated into writing curriculum is relevant as 56% of the teachers ranked digital games as "highly effective" (p. 49) in improving student learning in the subject area of ELA.

4.2 *Gaming and Writing*

Sabatino (2014) suggested videogaming and composition share common practices such as engagement, problem solving, and collaboration. Therefore, she used her experience with the Facebook game *Mafia Wars* to suggest how gaming and writing might be combined for use in the classroom. Johnson (2008) further discussed the writing gamers do in online communities as exercises in targeting audiences with specific writing purposes and that this writing was self-directed as well as collaborative. Some of the writing practices gamers participate in often go beyond the game itself including online journals, strategy guides, walk-throughs, fanfiction, blogs, websites, and gaming forums (Johnson, 2008).

4.3 *Relevant Theoretical Perspectives*

Jenkins et al. (2006) outlined the new media literacies necessary in what they defined as a participatory culture. A participatory culture is "a culture with relatively low barriers to artistic expression and civic engagement, strong support for creating and sharing one's creations, and some type of informal mentorship whereby what is known by the most experienced is passed along to novices" (Jenkins et al., 2006, p. 3). This culture values student creation versus the consumption of content that may be more typical in schools (see Hutchison, Woodward, & Colwell, 2016). To achieve such participation in an increasingly technological and globalized society (New London Group, 1996), Jenkins et al. (2006) argued that the following were necessary skills for students: problem solving through play, understanding multiple identities and perspectives, constructing real-world thinking, sampling and remixing content, multitasking, interacting with tools, sharing knowledge, evaluating information, navigating multiple modalities, and synthesizing information.

In his discussion of learning principles from gaming, Gee (2007) echoed some of the discussion of Jenkins et al. (2006) of needed skills in today's digital environment. For instance, Gee (2007) discussed gaming teaches that learning and literacy often entail making meaning through multimodality, "… images, texts, symbols, interactions, abstract design, sound, etc. … not just word" (p. 224). Gee (2007) and Jenkins et al. (2006) also agree that this learning is a social process. Whereas Jenkins et al. (2006) discussed this social nature of learning through new media literacy skills, such as collective intelligence and negotiation (p. 4), Gee (2007, p. 227) outlined the "Dispersed Principle," meaning that knowledge and meaning are something that learners share with others. In fact, in their more recent book (Jenkins et al., 2015), Jenkins and his colleagues revisit participatory culture and once again emphasize that this perspective emphasizes *both* creation and social learning. For example, highlighted in a chapter titled "Reimagining Participatory Culture," they emphasize, "participatory culture requires us to move beyond a focus on individualized personal expression; it is about an ethos of 'doing it together' in addition to 'doing it yourself'" (Jenkins et al., 2015, p. 181).

These scholars (Gee, 2007; Jenkins et al., 2006) similar to others before them (New London Group, 1996) emphasize that literacy is no longer about learning a standard form of language and expressing that form through only alphabetic text. Rather, literacy is about designing meaning through multimodality and social networks. Jenkins et al. (2006, 2015) emphasized that it is important to teach students this type of design as students may not have equitable access outside of school to the experiences with digital tools and networks that afford such design thinking, what they labeled the participation gap. Recent research, such as a survey of preadolescents by Hutchison et al. (2016), supports addressing this gap, as they found that although students had more access to digital tools and technologies in school than outside-of-school, this interaction was typically consuming media content rather than creating it, and these students struggled to recognize the legitimacy of digital forms of text and process multimodal information.

Thus, in the subsequent sections we will address how writing and gaming were conceptualized as literate practices during a NWP gaming camp. We will discuss how this camp combined writing and gaming to develop multimodality, social practice, and participatory culture through activities such as quick writes, games design, and collaboratively sharing this design.

5 Narrative of Context

The Youth Writing Camps (YWC) occurred as part of an official NWP site, located in the Southeast of the United States. Teacher consultants (TCs), teachers with NWP training, run the summer youth writing program offered for students from local school districts in grades 3–9. The Youth Writing Camps (YWC) consisted of three focal areas concentrated on developing the use of writing through various genres including scripts and game designs. These three focal areas include creative writing, film, and gaming. The Young Writers' Gaming Camp, the focus of this chapter, offers potential avenues for educators to infuse writing and technology within an ELA classroom through videogame design. In this program, campers design videogames focusing on specific elements of writing: choosing and designing settings, a story line, challenges, and characters.

In keeping with the NWP philosophy, the Young Writers' Gaming Camp is structured as a writing workshop. The key elements of the workshop include the following: quick writes, mini-lessons, writing time, and sharing. These elements are discussed in detail in the following sections. Table 1.1 provides an outline of the camp's daily schedule.

Although the general structure of the workshop remains the same from year to year, the materials and activities vary throughout. Table 1.2 provides an example of the camp at a weekly glance, including specific examples of quick writes, mini-lessons, writing time, and sharing. The workshop is situated in a computer lab, and all the writing is done digitally.

TABLE 1.1 Daily schedule

Timeframe	Workshop element	Description	Allocated minutes
09:00 AM	Quick Write	Campers begin the day with a quick write on blog page.	10 minutes
09:10 AM	Sharing	Campers share their quick writes with the group.	5 minutes
09:15 AM	Mini-Lesson	TC leads the group in a selected mini-lesson.	10 minutes
09:25 AM	Writing Time	Campers work independently to build games.	60 minutes
10:25 AM	Snack Break	Campers have snack and an opportunity to discuss their progress.	15 minutes
10:40 AM	Mini-Lesson	TC leads the group in a selected mini-lesson to introduce campers to a new type of gaming software.	10 minutes
10:50 AM	Writing Time	Campers work independently to build games.	30 minutes
11:20 AM	Share	Campers playtest each other's games.	15 minutes
11:35 AM	Writing Time	Campers use feedback to modify games.	10 minutes
11:45 AM	Quick Write	Campers end the day with a quick write on blog page.	10 minutes
11:55 AM	Wrap Up	Campers prepare for dismissal.	5 minutes

6 Practical Application: Activities Connecting Gaming and Writing

6.1 *Quick Writes and Finding Gaming Identity*

Campers started the day with a quick write in response to the provided prompt. This activity helps launch the mentality for writing and establishes a predictable routine to practice writing.

Campers used desktop computers to type their responses onto the camp website. Campers had an individualized blog page to account for their experience throughout the camp. Although the camp website is private, both past and present campers from all three focal areas have access to read one another's posts. Campers create avatars as visual representations of themselves for the blog page rather than first day of camp photographs. Avatars are either created using the Portrait Illustration Maker,[2] which generates pictures of

TABLE 1.2 Weekly schedule

Day	Topics of focus
M	– [Quick Write] What is your favorite game? Tell me everything you can about the game in as much detail as possible. – [Mini-Lesson] The Key Elements of Games – [Writing Time] Research: Games2U Video Game Theater (http://www.g2u.com/party/mobilepartytruck.php) – [Mini-Lesson] Game Design Challenge – [Writing Time] Game Design Challenge – [Sharing] Playtest Game Designs from Challenge and T.A.G. each team's design – [Quick Write] *Write a persuasive piece advertising your new game and persuading others to purchase it.*
T	– [Quick Write] *An important part of game design is research. Follow the link below to gather resources that will assist you in the production process. After conducting your research, write a brief summary of your findings. Which game did you enjoy the most? Discuss the key elements of the game: space, mechanics, components, goals, and rules.* https://www.atari.com/arcade – [Mini-Lesson] Introduction to Gamestar Mechanic http://gamestarmechanic.com – [Writing Time] Begin Quest, *Addison Joins the League* – [Mini-Lesson] Avatar Development: http://illustmaker.abi-station.com/index_en.shtml; http://www.voki.com/site/create – [Writing Time] Avatar Creations and continue Gamestar Mechanic quest – [Share] Upload Avatar Creations as profile picture for blog. – [Quick Write] *What I find easy about* Gamestar Mechanic/*What I find hard about* Gamestar Mechanic
W	– [Quick Write] *Yesterday I was able to do ______ and today my goal is to _______.* – [Mini-Lesson] Balancing the Key Elements and Avoiding Design Pitfalls https://www.youtube.com/watch?v=IUp8uRyoSZo – [Writing Time] Continue Quest and/or begin building Gamestar Mechanic game – [Mini-Lesson] Drag and Drop Programming: Introduction to Scratch – [Writing Time] Explore Scratch then work on building Gamestar Mechanic game – [Quick Write] *What was your experience like programming on* Scratch?

(*cont.*)

TABLE 1.2 Weekly schedule (*cont.*)

Day	Topics of focus
TR	– [Quick Write] Explain the storyline of your avatar. What is the background story behind your game? – [Mini-Lesson] Double Checking for Key Elements – [Writing Time] Continue building game – [Mini-Lesson] Introduction to Lightbot https://lightbot.com/hocflash.html – [Share] Playtest each others' game designs – [Quick Write] Based on the feedback you received from your playtester, what elements of your game did you revise and/or edit? Be specific. If you decided not to accept all the feedback, which parts did you ignore and why?
F	– [Quick Write] Write a persuasive piece advertising your Gamestar Mechanic game and persuading others to play/purchase it. – [Writing Time] Work on final touches of game and gaming research – [Share] Game Alley Arcade Event and Awards

customized characters or the Voki avatar software,[3] which generates talking customized characters.

On the first day of camp, campers wrote about their favorite game: *Why is this game their favorite? What is the game about? How does someone play the game?* This writing built community and provided the TCs an opportunity to discover how the campers identify as gamers. For example, campers might specify single/multiplayer, first person shooter, adventure, puzzle, action, role-playing, sports, etc. This quick write was used to prepare campers for learning and identifying the key elements of games by tapping into their prior knowledge. If the campers are able to recall their favorite games, it will be easier for them to learn and connect the new terminology with other games.

The quick writes were then used either to prepare campers for specific information that will be covered in a mini-lesson or as a reflection strategy at the end of the day. After campers researched classic games, the campers identified their favorite games by explaining elements of their design that they as players found enjoyable, aiding their future game design.

Just as writers read other mentor texts to improve their craft, gamers play other games to gather information and inspiration for their own creations, borrowing favorable elements and revising displeasing elements. These elements include *space* or the look of the game, *components* or the parts of the game, *mechanics* or actions of the game, *goals*, and *rules* for how the game should be played ("Gamestar," 2012).

In one quick write, campers reflected on their progress in the Gamestar Mechanic Quest: what was easy and what was hard. For example, Bryson (all names are pseudonyms) discussed how hard one level was to beat because of the restriction of time (rule) and the number of blocks (components) surrounding the goal. This particular prompt helped the TC to identify a possible focus for a mini-lesson and the progress of each camper. Most importantly, this quick write encouraged the campers to perform a self-assessment, building metacognitive awareness of their gaming identity.

6.2 *Mini-Lessons and Elements of Game Design*

This part of the workshop allowed the TCs to present a short lesson focused on a single topic to help campers with a particular skill in game development components. Some mini lessons were planned; some were derived through formative assessment such as conferencing.

For example, one of the first mini-lessons focused on identifying and defining the key elements of a game's design. It is pivotal; the campers understand the foundations of game design to then developed their own concepts. The TC introduced each term, asking campers to identify the elements in a particular game, one that is familiar to all the campers.

For example, the TC would ask two campers to demonstrate playing the game of Rock, Paper, Scissors. After a few rounds, the TC led the campers through an analysis of the various elements: *What is the goal of Rock, Paper, Scissors? Are there any rules or restrictions that players have to follow when playing Rock, Paper, Scissors? Where does the game take place: on a board, within a room?*

The Young Writers' Gaming Camp used a variety of software over the course of the program but focused upon the Gamestar Mechanic platform. The program used Gamestar Mechanic since its philosophy of teaching through play aligns with the philosophy of teaching and theoretical perspectives such as new media literacies from Jenkins et al. (2006). Instead of telling players about the various elements, Gamestar Mechanic shows the players these elements through completing a quest including several episodes with multiple missions. Each episode focuses on a different aspect of gaming. For example, Episode 4 is titled, "Gaining Perspective" because players learn the various factors of top-down versus platforming perspectives in games.

A top-down perspective provides the player with a bird's eye view of the space like Namco's 1980 original, *Pac-Man*.[4] A platformer perspective provides the player with a view of the space as if sliced from the side like Nintendo's

1985 original, *Super Mario Bros.*[5] Each perspective offers a uniquely different experience and is therefore an essential element to game design.

Once a day, TCs presented a different gaming software platform including Scratch,[6] Lightbot,[7] and a variety found from Hour of Code™[8] through their introduction to coding: *Atari Arcade* for historical gaming research, *Mars Generation One* for playtesting, and *Portal 2* for programming. When TCs introduced Scratch, for example, campers watched a brief video about *drag and drop* programming or coding. Coding is an important 21st century skill to which many students may not have access. Thus, it is important for teachers to provide authentic, equitable access to this type of participatory culture described by Jenkins et al. (2006). After the conclusion of the video, the TC introduced campers to the Scratch webpage and performed a brief demonstration of how the program works. The campers spent the next 10–20 minutes exploring the program on their own.

Once the camper initially explored the new software, he/she either would choose to continue working in the program or return to Gamestar Mechanic. In a quick write reflection, Jordan discussed the importance of Scratch as it allows individuals to see inside a game. Jordan expressed his concern that people take games for granted, not realizing the complexity of the software behind the scenes. Jordan enjoyed the freedom Scratch provides users when selecting sprites, controls, sounds, colors, etc. Most importantly, he enjoyed the community Scratch built for gamers.

6.3 *Social, Multimodal Design of Games*

The most important part of the workshop is writing time. This writing includes, but extends beyond, the conventional, text-based definition of writing to embrace multimodal design. As this type of writing, inclusive of multiple modes, may be new for the campers, it may require both more time as well as direction. Campers spent this part of the workshop working independently: drafting the storyline for their avatar, designing the space, selecting the components, editing the mechanics, revising the level and game messages, gathering information from mentor texts by playing in the Game Alley, exploring new concepts in the Quest, and playtesting another camper's game.

After the mini-lesson, the campers applied the information to their work. Sometimes the information from the mini-lesson was applied immediately by the camper. Other times the camper reserved the information until he/she needed the skill/tool. It was during this part of the workshop that the campers move recursively through the writing process.

While some campers were brainstorming the key elements of their game design, other campers were completing the first quest of Gamestar Mechanic to gain publishing rights, or they were in the Gamestar Mechanic workshop drafting the levels of their design, revising the game level messages to coincide with the rules and goals of their storyline, and editing the components or mechanics of the design to ensure players want to play their game. Campers also experienced game design as a process of social practice (Gee, 2007; Jenkins et al., 2006).

For example, one of the first mini-lessons was focused around the key elements of game design described previously. Campers were put into teams and challenged to create an original design from using only the provided materials. First, campers assessed the available components for developing their game. The components included items like paper clips, post-it notes, eraser heads, egg crates, coffee filters, straws, etc., and are varied for each group. After the team surveyed the components, they discuss and plan the game that they will develop including the mechanics, the goal, the rules, and the space. Campers must directly apply the key elements of game design discussed in the mini-lesson to complete the challenge. For this activity, campers drafted the key elements of their design, including the instructions on how to play, on a sheet of notebook paper. Although the camp primarily focused on producing videogames, this activity served an important role in teaching campers the concept of prototyping. The design challenge helped the campers apply the knowledge and skills they learned from the mini-lesson directly into a hands-on activity furthering their comprehension through application of the information and collaborative thinking.

Most of the writing time is spent designing and building the videogame. Writing in the Gamestar Mechanic workshop was different from the typical writing workshop. For example, drafting entailed campers selecting, building, designing, and adding new levels with various multimodal components. Campers revised level and game messages to incorporate the narrative of their avatar to develop the theme throughout the entire design. Editing took place when campers adjusted the mechanics of the included components, such as the speed or life value of an enemy. In addition, campers found inspiration from mentor texts in the form of playing other games. During this time, the TC conferenced with individual campers.

Even though working at home is not required, the majority of campers reported spending several more hours developing their games at home. Parents often remarked how surprised they were by the campers' enthusiasm and commitment to the development of the work. For example, Parker's parents confessed to finally having to take away the computer because she was working late into the evening.

6.4 *Collaborative Creation and Publication*

An essential part of the camp was the collaboration amongst campers. Campers learned early on that peer assessment is just as important as self-assessment. Designers created games because they wanted others to play them. This social element of game design is an invaluable concept to keep in mind throughout the design process, which was why campers continually playtest each other's games. Playtesting in the gaming workshop is like peer assessment in the writing workshop. A writing workshop environment encourages collaboration through seeking and providing feedback. This same concept was seen in the gaming workshop. The TC set up the concept of playtesting with a demonstration that captured the importance of T.A.G.-ing (Tell, Ask, Give) in a mini-lesson before the playtesting to strengthen the types of feedback received between groups. Campers learned by telling a positive comment, moving to ask a question to clarify details, and finally giving a constructive suggestion. All of the comments from T.A.G. require specific feedback, which was something the campers continued to improve upon throughout the week. This helps designers develop better games and continue to revise their design based on the feedback from the peers of their gaming community.

Students learned the value of providing thoughtful feedback in this community. In one quick write, Monica expressed her frustration when receiving feedback that was not specific enough to move her design forward. Students learned that comments such as "cool" or "this game was terrible" were not helpful feedback since they did not provide specific information as to what the player was experiencing. Colin explained how he edited his game based on feedback he received from another member in the Gamestar Mechanic community. Alex suggested he lower the difficulty of the game, and Colin responded by removing some sprites and editing the enemy sprites speed and damage. These are great examples of the skills the campers are acquiring through the social practice of gaming (Gee, 2007).

Campers had an opportunity to share all their hard work with friends and family at the game arcade finale. Similar to a writing workshop, the power of praise is important to building confidence amongst the community. It was not only important to celebrate the hard work and efforts put forth by the campers, but also it was imperative to allow them to exhibit this work to a more public audience. For the final two hours of the camp, parents, siblings, friends, grandparents, etc. join campers as they moved around the room to play the various designs created throughout the camp. Campers were typically excited to share their creations and visitors, of all gaming experience levels, were similarly eager to play. When a parent or sibling failed to beat a game, the camper was elated, as though this proved their mastery in design. This social engagement in the creation and publication of game design via digital tools put into practice what Jenkins et al. (2006) outlined in their theoretical perspective of participatory cultures.

7 Additional Resources

Teachers may want to investigate further some of the tools used in the camp: Voki, Gamestar Mechanic, and Scratch. Voki allows students to create an avatar that can talk through information they design, thus combining modes of images, text, and sound. Gamestar Mechanic[9] is a game-design platform for students in grades 4–9. This platform focuses on elements of game design rather than programming and allows students to share and comment on games collaboratively. Scratch is another gaming platform where students learn basic game programming by snapping together blocks with commands that control the game functionality and is intended for students from elementary through high school.

For a discussion on coding as a fundamental literacy, see Hutchison, Naldony, and Estapa (2015). Gaming as a participatory activity is important for all levels of literacy-elementary through secondary. For a discussion of how gaming can be integrated into secondary curriculum, see Herro (2015).

8 Conclusion

This one-week program offered campers an introduction to various online software systems to create their own video games and to join online gaming communities. Campers studied the elements of game design and worked collaboratively to authentically develop videogames that challenged their friends and family. Campers documented the process in a blog on the camp website while learning expectations for online etiquette and Internet safety. Throughout the program, campers explored the world of videogames, playtested mentor texts as models for videogame development, collaborated with peers throughout the process in person as well as online, and shared their products in an arcade event at the end of camp.

9 Connections and Questions

Key learnings from this chapter include the following: (a) gaming and writing are literacy practices that can be integrated to create a participatory culture in classrooms, (b) providing access to such participatory activities is necessary to create equitable opportunities for students to develop new media literacies, and (c) literacy is a social, multimodal practice that can be implemented in the classroom through activities such as quick writes, games design, and collaboratively sharing that design. There are questions that deserve further reflection: (a) How can gaming and writing be integrated to further literacy in disciplines other than ELA? (b) What scaffolds are needed to both introduce and bridge conventional and digital tools for gaming? and (c) How can the concepts of writing workshop and games design illustrated in this camp environment be integrated effectively into K-12 classrooms?

Notes

1. The NWP is a national organization that provides professional development to teachers, specifically focused on writing (www.nwp.org).
2. http://illustmaker.abi-station.com/index_en.shtml
3. http://www.voki.com
4. https://pacman.com/
5. https://mario.nintendo.com/
6. https://scratch.mit.edu
7. https://lightbot.com
8. https://code.org/learn
9. https://gamestarmechanic.com/

References

Alberti, J. (2008). The game of reading and writing: How video games reframe our understanding of literacy. *Computers and Composition, 25*(3), 258–269.

Carter, S., Greenberg, K, & Walker, M. (2016). *The impact of computer usage on academic performance: Evidence from a randomized trial at The United States Military Academy* (Working Paper). National Bureau of Economic Research.

Duggan, M. (2015). *Gaming and gamers*. Washington, DC. Pew Research Center's Internet & American Life Project. Retrieved from http://www.pewinternet.org/2015/12/15/gaming-and-gamers/

Gamestar Mechanic: Getting started teacher pack. (2012). [Online]. Retrieved from http://cdn2.gamestarmechanic.com/static-1671/pdfs/gamestar-getting-started-pack.pdf

Gee, J. P. (2007). *What video games have to teach us about learning and literacy*. New York, NY: Palgrave Macmillan.

Herro, D. (2015). Gaming the system: Culture, process, and perspectives supporting a game and app design curriculum. *The Curriculum Journal, 26*(4), 579–600.

Hutchison, A., Naldony, L., & Estapa, A. (2016). Using coding apps to support literacy instruction and develop coding literacy. *The Reading Teacher, 69*(5), 493.

Hutchison, A., & Reinking, D. (2011). Teachers' perceptions of integrating information and communication technologies into literacy instruction: A national survey in the United States. *Reading Research Quarterly, 46*(4), 312–333.

Hutchison, A. C., Woodward, L., & Colwell, J. (2016). What are preadolescent readers doing online? An examination of upper elementary students' reading, writing, and communication in digital spaces. *Reading Research Quarterly, 51*(4), 435–454.

Jenkins, H., Clinton, K., Purushotma, R., Robison, A., & Weigel, M. (2006). *Confronting the challenges of participatory culture: Media education for the 21st century white paper*. MacArthur Foundation.

Jenkins, H., Ito, M., & boyd, d. (2015). *Participatory culture in a networked era: A conversation on youth, learning, commerce, and politics*. Cambridge: Polity Press.

Johnson, M. S. S. (2008). Public writing in gaming spaces. *Computers and Composition, 25*(3), 270–283.

Means, B., & Peters, V. (2016, April). *Influences on the scaling of digital learning resources*. Paper presentation at the 2016 American Education Research Associational Conference, Washington, DC.

New London Group (NLG). (1996). A pedagogy of multiliteracies: Designing social futures. *Harvard Education Review, 66*, 60–92.

Peterson, S. S., & McClay, J. K. (2012). Assumptions and practices in using digital technologies to teach writing in middle-level classrooms across Canada. *Literacy, 46*(3), 140–146.

Sabatino, L. (2014). Improving writing literacies through digital gaming literacies: Facebook gaming in the composition classroom. *Computers and Composition: An International Journal for Teachers of Writing, 32*, 41–53.

Takeuchi, L. M., & Vaala, S. (2014). *Level up learning: A national survey on teaching with digital games*. New York: The Joan Ganz Cooney Center at Sesame Workshop.

CHAPTER 2

Time to Level Up: Learning through Play in a Writing Classroom

Rachel Kaminski Sanders

1 Overarching Questions

1. How does the inclusion of play promote increased engagement and critical learning amongst students?
2. What are the types of writing required in designing and building video games?
3. How can gaming encourage collaboration in a writing community?

2 Introduction

> Play is often talked about as if it were a relief from serious learning. But for children, play is serious learning. Play is really the work of childhood. (Fred Rogers)

There are varieties of games that exist in today's society but the educational outlook on the term is quite the same: gaming and learning do not belong together. Most educational institutions believe there are not enough hours in the school day for students to "play", which is something that needs to be done at home. However, much like Mister Rogers, I found that play has an important place inside the classroom. In this article, I will discuss how the inclusion of play through gaming promotes both increased engagement and critical learning amongst students.

3 Academic Disconnect: Statement of Problem

Technological advancements have brought changes that were never before imaginable. For example, in the seventh grade, I did not have a cell phone. Even my parents did not own one at the time. When my teachers wanted to use technology in the classroom, the librarian would wheel down the cart with

 | DOI: 10.1163/9789004422315_004

one of the three TVs the school possessed. That was back in 1998. The amount of change since then – two decades later – is almost unbelievable.

According to a report by Internet Live Stats (2017), only 43.1% of the United States population were using the Internet in the year 2000. It would be fair to say that during that time everyday use of technology was not a common practice amongst members of society. That percentage has doubled in just the past two decades. As of 2016, 88.5% of the US population are using the Internet (Internet Live Stats, 2017). The majority of adolescents own at least one piece of technology if not more. When it was once rare to have cell phones in a home, it is now more rare to see a telephone, also known as a landline, within a household (Blumberg & Luke, 2016). Even with all the advancements of the past 20 years, some educators complain cell phones are a distraction in the classroom and enforce strict policies that greatly restrict the use of technological devices (Lenhart, Ling, Campbell, & Purcell, 2010).

To literacy educators, like Alvermann and Hagood (2000), Gee (2016), and Rushkoff (2013), it is increasingly clear that the current system of education is failing our students, simply because the current system of education is not, in fact, current. If technology is limited within the walls of school, how are students to prepare for life outside of the school? The world is quickly changing, and technology is a major reason. Educational systems have failed to move forward from the age of the assembly lines to better prepare students to become the future workers of society (Davidson, 2011). Because schools continue with an old pattern of learning, Davidson (2011) argues, they are no longer preparing students for the new intellectual habits of this generation, thereby, diminishing the opportunities for students to flourish in the digital literacies of today. Society has to learn how to live with these technological developments including the new literacy practices produced from these advancements, emphasizing the importance of bringing technology inside the classroom.

3.1 *Making the Connection: A Possible Solution*

So, what needs to happen to close the gap between real world practices and classroom practices? Educators need to take a more proactive, rather than passive, approach to education. It is time for the education system to level up! Students are becoming experts in various places outside of the classroom and it is imperative to bring their knowledge and interest into the classroom in order to promote authentic learning and critical thinking.

Rather than remaining consumers of information, students need to be actively engaged producers that today's society needs. One way to create twenty-first century classrooms is to include game-based learning, specifically with videogames. According to James Gee, Professor of Literary Studies in Digital Media and Learning, "The purpose of games as learning (and other game-like forms of learning) should be to make every learner a proactive, collaborative, reflective, critical, creative, and innovative problem solver; a producer with technology and not just a consumer; and a fully engaged participant and not just a spectator in civic life and the public sphere" (2013, p. 1). Like the Internet, the principles of gaming incorporate multimodal literacies, promote nonlinear patterns of thinking, and allow the interconnectivity of present culture, which are essential components to learning in the 21st century (Gee, 2013; Rushkoff, 2013).

3.2 *Narrative of Context*

During my first year of teaching 7th grade writing, students were expected to produce a brochure about a selected topic to demonstrate the mastery of an informational genre. The project reminded me of an assignment I once completed in the seventh grade, when technology wasn't as commonplace both inside and outside the classroom. That can no longer be said. I could not imagine how this project would be relevant to today's students who were communicating on their personal cell phones. With reluctance, I followed the assigned unit fearful of the consequences otherwise, a conflict often faced by first-year teachers. Students simply went through the motions to complete the assignment. We could not wait for it to be over.

Later that same year, I attended the National Writing Project annual conference in Las Vegas, Nevada. At one of the seminars, I was introduced to *Gamestar Mechanic* (2010). At the time I was interested in gaming for a summer youth camp with the Upstate Writing Project (Howell & Sanders, Part 4 Chapter 1). Without the pressures of classroom teaching, I felt more freedom to attempt the *Gamestar Mechanic* software with the campers. The campers worked hard on their videogame design projects inside the classroom but more importantly, they continued to work on it outside of the camp sessions. Imagine a summer camp where the students were completing "homework" at home. Willingly.

Not surprisingly, in my second year of teaching, I had grown a little more confident with challenging district prescribed units. I knew, based on the camper experiences, I could support my decision with evidence of students' learning. Therefore, I decided against using the brochure assignment as the required informational unit of study. In its place, I incorporated gaming.

Instead of dreading the second nine weeks, I was hoping that by throwing out the brochure and picking up the gaming unit, my students would be more actively engaged. Rather than simply completing the assignment because the teacher said so, I hoped the students would take ownership of the project just as the campers did that past summer.

3.3 *Introduction to Informational Writing of Instruction*

We began the second nine week's unit by discussing various forms of informational writing, including: menus, brochures, instructions, charts/graphs and maps. We then discussed which of the formats most frequently appear in real life settings. Students identified giving/receiving instructions or providing directions as a vital informational tool to everyday life applications.

After the students identified the potential use and importance of the type of writing, the students needed time to explore the mechanics of the writing for themselves. The students were asked to bring in an object, any object of their choice, for the following day's lesson. No further guidelines were provided. The suspense of the unknown had the students already giddy with excitement.

Seated in rows the following day, the students placed the selected object on top of their desk. I too shared my own object, a roll of toilet paper, which not surprisingly was a big hit with a seventh-grade audience. Two requirements for being a middle school teacher include having tough skin and having a good sense of humor … of the potty variety. The class discussed the use of directions with the popular series "How to … for Dummies" and I modelled an example on the board with my object. Seemingly simple enough, the students wrote down the instructions for how to use their selected object at their desk.

After allowing a few minutes to write, I provided the students with the next set of directions. Students would rotate around to different seats. At each new seat, the students were to follow the provided instructions exactly as written. For example, a student that wrote directions for using lip-gloss simply instructed the user to "put the lip gloss on". As the fellow student followed the provided instructions exactly as stated, the student placed the lip-gloss "on" their lap. Therefore, the writer discovered the importance of clarifying exact instructions such as, "After removing the cap, rub the glossy end on your lips to cover the dry areas".

This process turned out to be quite humorous as students were using everyday items incorrectly and through which, discovered the importance of providing specific and clear instructions to their readers. Now that the students understood the importance of clear and specific directions, the unit was beginning to take form and the students were ready for the primary focus of the unit, writing informational texts through gaming.

3.4 *Introduction to Gaming*

The students were aware of the importance of providing instructions but still did not know the format in which the instructions would focus for the unit. Therefore, the next step of the unit was to introduce the complex and historical background of gaming, and this is where the unit got exciting. Videogames were in the classroom and students could not believe it. Most were jumping out of their seats with joy.

Through a brief overview to gaming with a Prezi presentation, students were introduced to key terms and elements of gaming, a timeline of videogames, the economic profits of being a game developer, statistical information about gamers including hard-core vs. casual gamers, gaming market places, the future of the gaming industry, and the longevity of game design.

Since students would be developing the final product on *Gamestar Mechanic*, the unit followed the program's essential elements of game design including goal, rules, space, mechanics and components. Table 2.1 provides a brief overview of the terms and definitions built upon throughout the unit.

3.5 *Analysis of Game Elements*

With their toes in the water, the unit could begin to build into hands-on activities. Students knew the meaning of the key terms but now they needed to put those terms into application. The class divided into groups and each group

TABLE 2.1 Key terms of game design unit

Element	Definition
Balance	the game gradually increases with difficulty to narrow the amount of successful players
Components	the parts of the game, sprites
Gamestar Mechanic	online community that teaches students how to build and design videogames
Goals	what players try to achieve in order to win the game
Mechanics	the actions in the game like jumping or collecting
Quest	a narrative adventure shown in motion comics and mini-games
Rules	guide the player on how the game should be played
Space	the look and feel of a game design
Sprites	computer image or graphic

SOURCE: ADAPTED FROM E-LINE MEDIA & THE INSTITUTE OF PLAY (2010).

received a board game. Students were to apply their knowledge to identify the core elements of the game design using the vocabulary introduced during the previous class period. At the end of the class, students provided a brief overview of their findings to the rest of the class. The activity assessed the students understanding and identification of the core game elements, moving past a preliminary memorization of the terms' meaning into higher order thinking skills through the application of the terms to real life examples.

3.6 *Application of Game Elements*

The students were ready for the next challenge, with the core elements of game design in mind; students were to work in teams to design and build their very own game. The students formed self-selected groups and received a bin full of various objects and resources. For example, one bin contained 20 paper clips, five eraser heads, four toys, six pipe cleaners of various colors, a brown paper lunch bag, a sleeve of star stickers, a pack of markers, two large foam dice, and one large post-it note shaped like a star. Each group had access to an infinite amount of dot matrix computer paper, the continuous kind with perforated edges on both sides. In Figure 2.1, the students are pictured analyzing the provided materials and planning their game's design based on the terms developed from the five essential elements.

FIGURE 2.1 Game design challenge, planning

The groups had two class periods to design and create an original game using only the supplies provided. The groups could use all or as little of the supplies as they preferred. Each group produced a set of instructions for how the game was played as well as identified the five core components of game design: the goal, rules, space, components, and mechanics of the game.

Students were also asked to create an original title based on the theme of the game and that the theme be clearly present throughout all the components of the game. The groups discussed the theme, the title, and the elements of design from the mentor text, the already existent board games, as a guide to their final product. Figure 2.2 shows students designing and creating their game. This step of the process often involved students bending, stretching, twisting, pulling, deconstructing, and attaching the various materials until the desired outcome achieved, like scientists conducting an experiment.

On the third day of the activity, the groups were to layout the instructions with the identified elements but not to assemble the game board. The groups rotated from game to game in order to assemble and play each game by utilizing the provided instructions and elements. After a period to play, the groups

FIGURE 2.2 Game design challenge, creating

FIGURE 2.3 Game design challenge, playing

went around the room to provide positive feedback as well as constructive feedback to the game designers. The game designers then returned to their game and made the appropriate revisions.

Figure 2.3 captures a student playtesting another group's game design. The goal of the game was to stack wooden blocks, of decreasing size, onto a popsicle stick. The player must balance the popsicle stick in one hand while using the other to add to the remaining items. To win, the player must balance all the wooden blocks on the stick after adding the large pink dice on top for 5 seconds without collapsing. In order to make the game more challenging, the playtester suggested explicitly stating in the rules that the wooden blocks must form a single column, as spreading the blocks horizontally over the popsicle stick would make the task quite easier. The original designers had not previously thought of this strategy by the player and revised the rules in order to address this area of the game.

Now that they understood the requirements of effective game design, the students could move forward with the next part of the unit. Not only did the students synthesize and work hands on with the core elements of game design, the students also participated in playtester feedback, playing another's game to provide feedback on how the game might be improved, a vital role in game development as well as the writing process. Figure 2.4 includes two examples of the games produced as a final product from the game design challenge activity. The majority of the game spaces used the properties of dot matrix paper to advance their designs: extending or limiting the length of the game's

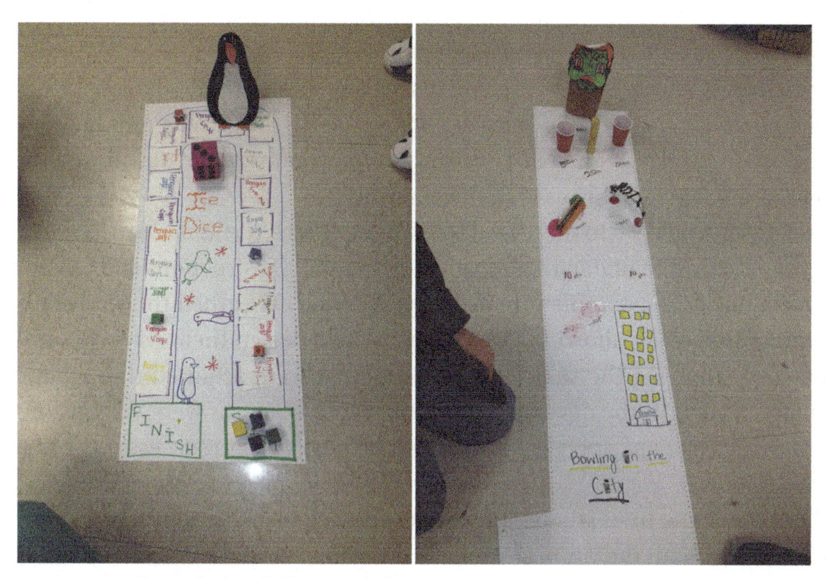

FIGURE 2.4 Game design challenge, products

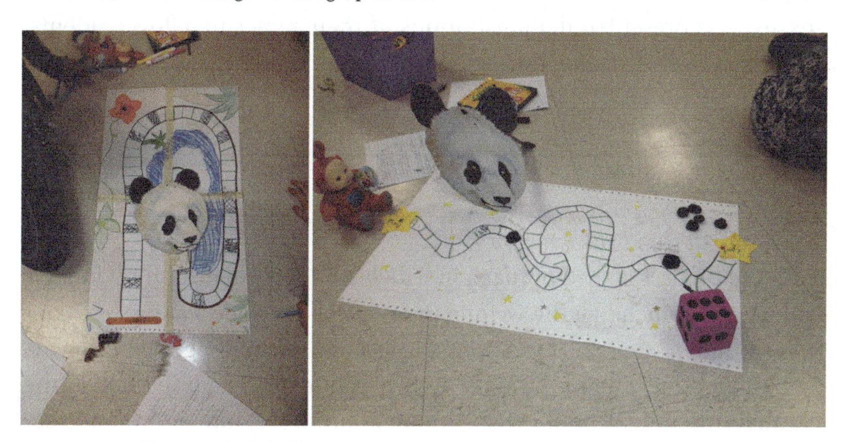

FIGURE 2.5 Game design challenge, variations

board. However, several of the game spaces were not restricted to a board, like the example in Figure 2.3, and used various properties of the classroom space, like the wall or the back of a chair.

Although groups from one class period to the next received the same bin of materials, the designs the students created were continually unique and original. Figure 2.5 comprises two games produced in two different class periods, completely different students, using the same materials. The panda in the first design is used as part of the game's mechanics, how the player moves, and the panda in the second game is used as an element of design to further the theme of the game.

3.7 *Application of the Idea: The Project*

After analyzing and applying the elements of game design in the challenge, students were ready for the *Gamestar Mechanic* project. The gaming unit focused on both giving and providing instructions, a type of informational writing that is consistently and reliably used in the real world.

Students would need to successfully complete Quest 1 on *Gamestar Mechanic* by demonstrating an understanding of both providing instructions and following directions. Upon completion of the quest, students earned the workshop publishing privileges, allowing them to create and design their very own videogames by applying the skills and concepts that were acquired throughout the quest. As part of the development of the game, students were responsible for providing clear and specific instructions to the players to successfully complete the game.

Throughout the unit, students received peer feedback to adjust and guide their thinking about the various elements of a game. At the end of the unit, the classroom became an active game arcade. Students engaged in each other's designs, experts presented demonstrations of their games to fellow students, and all were actively learning through play.

4 Project Components

4.1 *Game Design Process*

Game design process is the approach in which students create and build their own videogame. Much like the writing process, the game design process consists of five major areas of focus: preparing/brainstorming, designing, playtesting and iterating, and publishing. In this section, I take a brief look at the process that my students and I went through during this interactive informational unit.

4.2 *Preparing*

The first step of the game design process was preparation. Students needed to understand the ins and outs of the game design elements. In "Addison Joins the League", the first quest on *Gamestar Mechanic*, students learned the mechanics of game design through play in order to become a master game designer.

Before beginning, the students were guided through an interactive graphic novel that establishes the storyline of the avatar and the context of the quest. Students, through the avatar Addison, work towards mastering various gaming skills thinking as both a designer as well as a player in order to become a League mechanic. As Addison progresses through the quest, the graphic novel is interwoven throughout the missions to advance the storyline and development of the plot.

Throughout the first quest, students must play their way through the game-based instruction. In the process, students obtain the required knowledge to design, create, repair, and produce a game. At times, students simply master the components of the game-like learning to use a jumping avatar to increase game complexity or face the challenge of restricted lives. At other times, students fix a broken game, demonstrating an understanding of the tools available for creation.

Students must design and develop their first game in the final mission of the first quest called, "Clean Slate". Using the knowledge accumulated throughout the first quest, students must successfully produce a game that meets the required specifications of the mission. Once the game design meets the requirements, students must beat the developed game in order for it to be publishable. If the student cannot complete the game, they must keep trying until completion or return to the editing mode to reformat the game in order for it to be beatable. This is a very important part of *Gamestar Mechanic*; all published games are beatable.

The successful completion of "Clean Slate" mission in the first quest earns the player the *League Mechanic* badge and unlocks the rights to publishing games in the workshop. This ensures students have mastered the concepts of game design and are capable of producing a game for all to share. Much like conducting research, this part of the project supported students in the development of their own ideas for game design. Students were challenged in the "Addison Joins the League" quest to look at each of the gaming elements in different ways in order to see how the modification of an element affected other parts of the game.

4.3 *Brainstorming*

After the successful completion of the "Addison Joins the League" quest, students were ready to start designing their very own game. In order to give the game more purpose, students planned their designs around the guidelines of the annual *Scholastic Art and Writing Awards* in order to submit the final project in the contest. The guidelines included: an interactive media experience, playable games, originality, technical skills, and personal vision (Scholastic, 2014). Scholastic (2014) outlined technical skills using the following specifications:

1. Clear instructions so the player know what they should be trying to do;
2. A story or reason for the avatar to do what it is going to do, told through the Game Intro, Game Win Message, and the Level Intros;
3. Gameplay that relates to the story;

4. Carefully chosen sprites, background and music that help set the game scene.

Keeping in mind the concept of the quest as a mentor text; students identified the essential elements of their game design including a theme selection. Figure 2.6 illustrates the graphic organizer students used throughout the prewriting process in order to think through each of the essential traits in gaming, as well as a student sample. The remainder of the chapter showcases the progression of this particular student's project, *Winter Race*, throughout the game writing process.

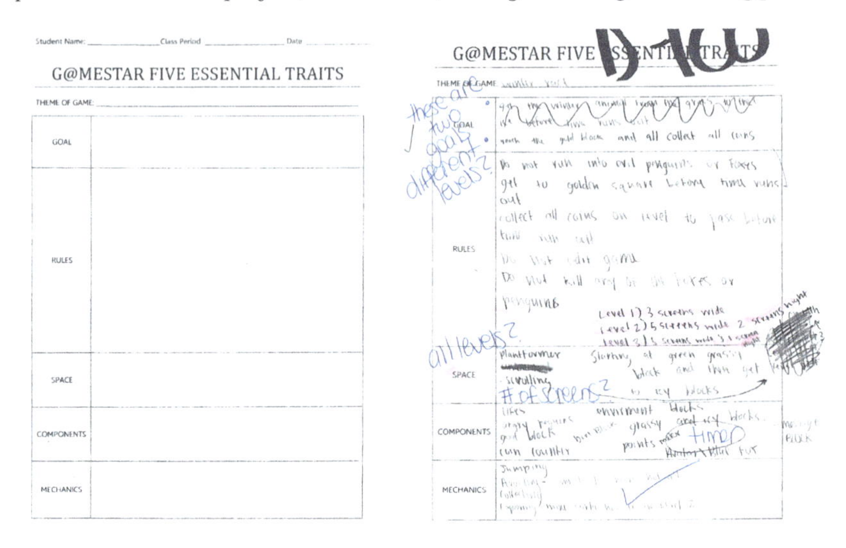

FIGURE 2.6 Gamestar Mechanic prewriting graphic organizer

Additionally, the students explored the available sprites, a computer image or graphic, for inspiration on the development of their theme. A few students created original narratives based around a selected avatar. For the particular example shown in Figure 2.6, the fox sprite inspired the *Winter Race* story, based on survival from the harsh elements of winter. Other students brought narratives from popular TV shows and book series to life. For example, one student designed a game based on *Jurassic Park* utilizing the dinosaur sprites from the *AMD Impact Challenge*. Students were not only working on the instructions of how to play the game, but they were also incorporating elements they learned from a narrative unit in the previous nine weeks such as character development, plot, setting, dialogue, etc.

4.4 *Designing*

Once the students narrowed down the focus of their game, they could begin building the project. Students utilized the brainstorming organizer as a blueprint and kept in mind the question, "what do your design choices mean for the player?", allowing them to make meaningful selections of specific components and sprites. When drafting the game and level settings, students focused on providing clear and specific instructions to the players. Throughout all elements of the game design, the students interwove the theme in order to make the avatar's role purposeful. Figure 2.7 includes the original drafting map students used to write the context of their games. Additionally, the progression of *Winter Race* from the initial thinking in the graphic organizer (see Figure 2.6) is developed here in the draft. The student furthers the narrative by establishing the problem faced by the avatar: if the snow fox cannot make it back to the snow, the fox will die. This establishes a connection between the avatar and the space. The environment directly affects the animals' survival, similar to that found in nature.

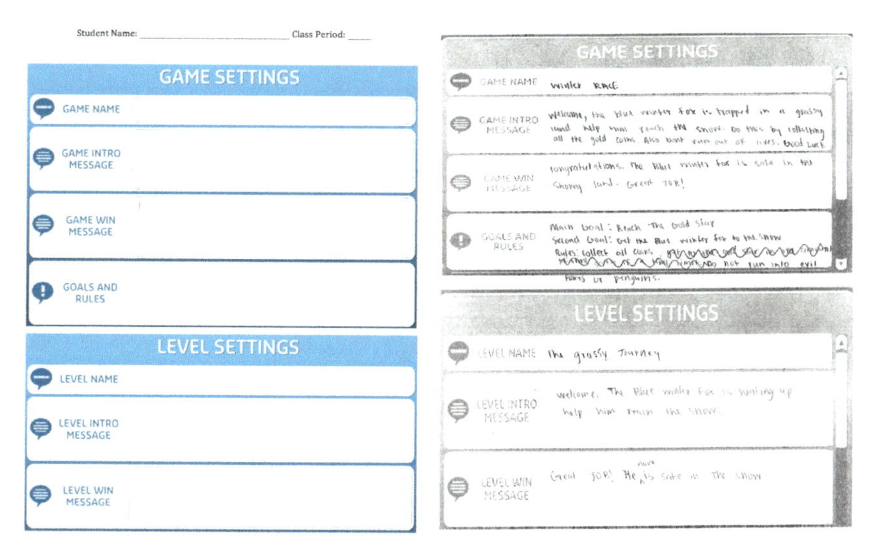

FIGURE 2.7 Gamestar Mechanic drafting map

4.5 *Playtesting and Iterating*

Playtesting is a major part of game design. The final product distributed worldwide did not make its way into the customers' hands without first going through an extensive process of peer feedback. Peer feedback is one of the biggest areas of improvement for students. Typically, most students find the writing process of revising and editing unnecessary. However, the inclusion of playtesting in this unit proved otherwise. Students actively asked others to play their game either to prove that their game was the best or if the player beat the game too easily, the designer would immediately return to the development stage.

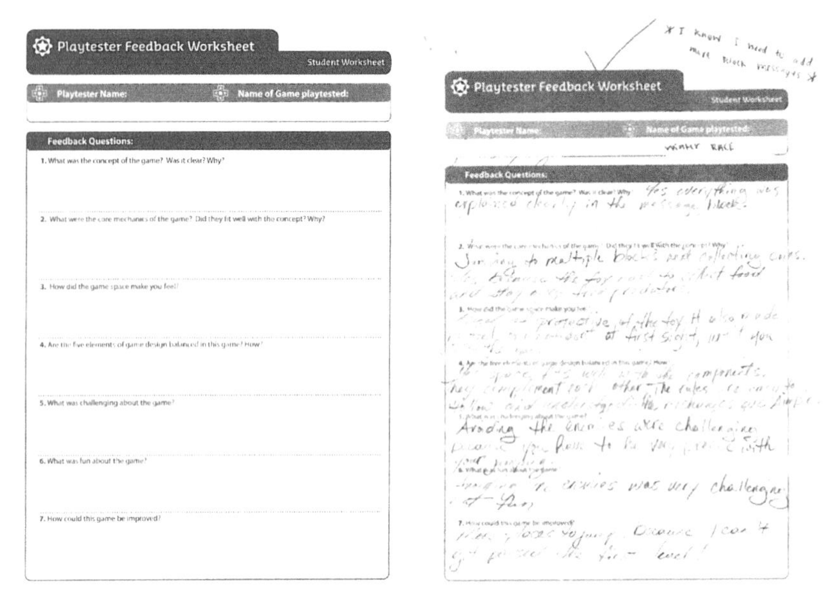

FIGURE 2.8 Playtester feedback form

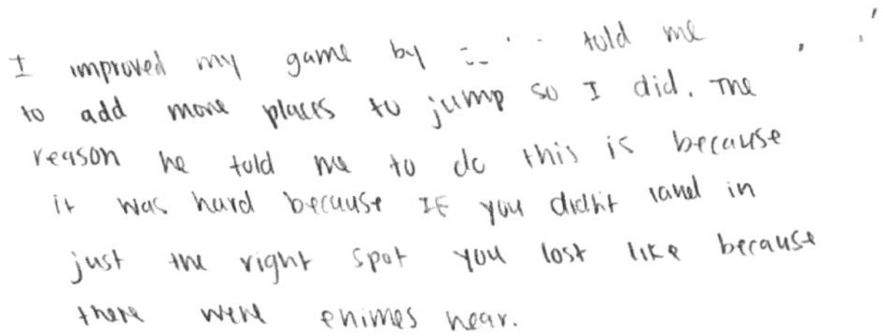

I improved my game by -- told me to add more places to jump so I did. The reason he told me to do this is because it was hard because If you didn't land in just the right spot you lost like because there were enimes near.

FIGURE 2.9 Gamestar Mechanic description of iteration based on playtester feedback

Since students were already engaging in playtesting, I asked the students to record their feedback after playing each other's games on the feedback worksheet provided on the *Gamestar Mechanic* (2010) website. Figure 2.8 captures the playtester feedback for *Winter Race* in which the player indicates a problem with the balance of how the game is played.

After receiving the playtester feedback, students iterated the writing process by revising and editing the games based on the provided suggestions. Students were asked to write a brief description of the changes that were implemented because of the playtester feedback. Figure 2.9 is the *Winter Race* designer's description of the iteration process from the playtester feedback. Here the designer was addressing the problem identified during playtesting: the player found it too difficult to enjoy playing. Balance is often the hardest element to design. Players want a challenge but not an impossibility.

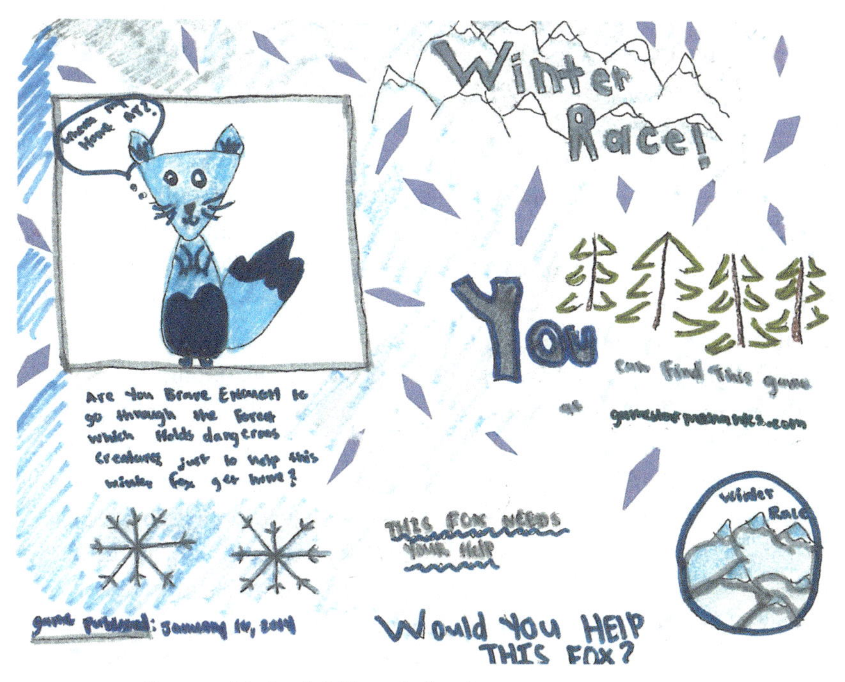

FIGURE 2.10 Gamestar Mechanic billboard advertisement

4.6 *Publishing*

Although, students were excited about submitting their completed designs to the annual *Scholastic Art and Writing Awards*, the class was most excited about Arcade Day; the class period after the project deadline was the main event. In preparation for Arcade Day, students created billboard advertisements to display in the hallway of the school to encourage others to visit their games. Figure 2.10 shows an example of one of the advertisements that was developed by the designer of *Winter Race*. This part of the project provided a small glimpse into the elements of the next unit of study, persuasive writing. Students had both a personal and realistic reason for using persuasion in order to attract players to their designs. Students across grade levels were participating in the games, building an even stronger connection to a real-life audience.

Students spent the entire class period playing one another's games. In addition, students were encouraged to bring other gaming systems to share their expertise. This meant that in one corner of the room, a student might be demoing *Madden Football*. On the Smartboard, another student demoed *Minecraft* or *Portal 2*. Students eagerly shared their expertise with the rest of the class. At one point, a student was the teacher and in the next, an active learner.

5 Conclusion

Much like McGonigal (2011), my students found games to be instrumental to their development and growth. Videogames engage players in an open-ended fashion, they communicate through experience instead of telling, and they invite players into the creative process. Bringing popular culture, like gaming, into the classroom allows students to engage with the skills needed to survive the 21st century and beyond, through the most important connections, they can make; their personal lives.

Pushback from educators over the use of play in the classroom stems partly from the worry about the limited time and space for already overly planned school curricula. In "Being in the Moment: Implications for Teaching and Young People's Digital Literacies", Alvermann (2015) argued that games "offer an alternative to traditional instruction by providing youth with a potentially active role in their own learning" (p. 626). Play becomes the vehicle that allows students to learn through, not instead of. The 21st century classroom will consist of "moving from worlds inhabited by many of the kinds of characters and roles" in games "to worlds inhabited by scientists, historians, ecologists, physicist, urban planners, geographers, biologists, and so on" (Knobel & Lankshear, 2008, pp. 30–31). Gaming provides the learning skills that extend beyond the classroom into real world settings.

I found that a classroom environment that promotes learning through play opens an environment where students are free to critically explore and tinker as independent learners without fear of failure. When a student failed a quest, they got right back into the game, never giving up and trying again repeatedly until the game was won. If a student were stuck, they would actively seek help from peers. Students were actively engaging in the writing process, building a community of lifelong learners and engaging in complex literacy skills to develop an idea from paper to computer screen. The inclusion of play in the classroom promoted both increased engagement and critical learning amongst students. For the first time in a long time, students were playing, rather than pretending, to learn.

References

Addison Joins the League: First Quest – Learning Guide. (n.d.). Retrieved November 29, 2015, from https://sites.google.com/a/elinemedia.com/gsmlearningguide/online-learning-guide-resources/quest-guide/addison-joins-the-league

Alvermann, D. E. (2015). Being in the moment: Implications for teaching and young people's digital literacies. *Journal of Adolescent & Adult Literature, 58*(8), 625–631.

Alvermann, D. E., & Hagood, M. C. (2000). Critical media literacy: Research, theory, and practice in "new times." *Journal of Educational Research, 93*, 193–205.

Blumberg, S. J., & Luke, J. V. (2016, May). Wireless substitution: Early release of estimates from the National Health Interview Survey, July–December 2015. *National Center for Health Statistics*, 1–13. Retrieved from https://www.cdc.gov/nchs/data/nhis/earlyrelease/wireless201605.pdf

Davidson, C. (2011). *Now you see it: How the brain science of attention will transform the way we live, work, and learn.* New York, NY: Viking Press.

E-line Media & the Institute of Play. (2010). *Gamestar mechanic* [Online video game]. University of Wisconsin-Madison: Gamelab.

Gee, J. (2013). *Good video games and good learning: Collected essays on video games, learning and literacy.* London: Peter Lang.

Gee, J. (2016). *A conversation with James Gee.* Clemson University, Watt Family Innovation Center, Clemson, SC. March 31. Keynote Address.

Internet Live Stats. (2017). *United States internet users.* Retrieved from http://www.internetlivestats.com/internet-users/us/

Kennedy, K., & Molen, G. R. (Producers), & Spielberg, S. (Director). (1993, June 11). *Jurassic Park* [Motion picture]. United States: Universal Pictures.

Knobel, M., & Lankshear, C. (2008). Remix: The art and craft of endless hybridization. *Journal of Adolescent & Adult Literacy, 52*(1), 22–33.

Lenhart, A., Ling, R., Campbell, S., & Purcell, K. (2010, April). Teens and mobile phones: Text messaging explodes as teens embrace it as the centerpiece of their communication strategies with friends. *Pew Internet & American Life Project*, 1–114. Retrieved from http://www.pewinternet.org/files/old-media//Files/Reports/2010/PIP-Teens-and-Mobile-2010-with-topline.pdf

McGonigal, J. (2011). *Reality is broken.* New York, NY: The Penguin Press.

Moore, H. (2014, September 23). *Why play is the work of childhood – Fred Rogers center for early learning & children's media.* Retrieved November 29, 2015, from http://www.fredrogerscenter.org/2014/09/23/why-play-is-the-work-of-childhood/

Rushkoff, D. (2013). *Present shock: When everything happens now.* New York, NY: The Penguin Group.

Scholastic Art Writing Awards Categories. (2014). Retrieved November 30, 2015, from http://www.artandwriting.org/the-awards/categories/#24

CHAPTER 3

Gaming the System: Engaging Students in the Imaginative Worlds of Young Adult Literature through Role-Playing Games

Lindy L. Johnson and Elizabeth DeBoeser

1 Overarching Questions

1. How can role-playing game help students create immersive and imaginative literary worlds?
2. How do role-playing games provide students with opportunities to connect and extend their out of school literacy practices around gaming?
3. What role-playing activities do you already incorporate into your teaching of literature? How might you extend these activities so that students are given opportunities to experience the aesthetic aspects of reading?
4. What are some of your and your students' favorite games? How might you adapt aspects of these games into your teaching of reading and writing?
5. What do you see as the benefits and challenges of creating a participatory culture in your classroom?

2 Introduction

> Honestly, I feel I could have read the book a thousand times over and like studied it a bunch, but I wouldn't have felt like as absorbed in it as I do right now. Because I'm actually *in* the world. And, I'm having to make decisions as if I were the characters. (Aidan, a 6th grade student in Elizabeth's class)

In describing that what it was like to create and play an RPG game based on the novel *My Brother Sam is Dead*, Aidan focused on the immersive and imaginative world he and his peers created. Aidan's comments were representative of other students who talked often about inhabiting the worlds of their novels. One of the primary purposes of teaching literature is to help students understand how to inhabit worlds not their own and to take on perspectives

 | DOI: 10.1163/9789004422315_005

of characters different from their own. When we encourage students to inhabit worlds not their own, we are foregrounding the aesthetic aspects of Rosenblatt's transactional theory of reading (Rosenblatt, 1994/2005c) where readers "focus attention on what is being lived through during the reading event" (p. 11). This aesthetic element is often missing in reading instruction but is a necessary component if we want students to engage meaningfully with texts.

In this chapter, we focus on the ways a participatory culture was created in a 6th grade English Language Arts (ELA) classroom through an immersive historical fiction unit where students participated in book clubs and created role-playing games (RPGs). This interdisciplinary unit focused on the political and social landscape of the American Revolution. Students could choose to read one of three young adult novels, *Chains* (Anderson, 2008), *My Brother Sam is Dead* (Collier & Collier, 1974), or *Sophia's War: A Tale of Revolution* (Avi, 2012). For their final project, students created a role-playing game (RPG) based on their chosen novel. RPGs refer to games where players take on the role of imaginary characters that participate in various adventures facilitated by a Game Master (GM).

3 Game-Based Learning and Literacy

Many researchers have theorized the potential of game-based learning to enhance student learning in schools (Gee, 2007, Abrams, 2009; Gerber & Price, 2011). For example, Gee (2007) argued that videogames have much to teach those of us who care about learning and literacy. Researchers have found that young people learn a great deal through their participation in digitally-mediated informal learning spaces (Ito, 2010). These learning spaces are characterized by participatory cultures where there are 1) relatively low barriers to artistic expression and civic engagement; 2) strong support for creating and sharing creations with others; 3) some type of informal mentorship; 4) members who feel that their contributions matter; and 5) members who feel some degree of social connection to one another (Jenkins, Purushotoma, Weigel, Clinton, & Robison, 2009, pp. 5–6). English teachers often talk about the importance of creating a community of readers and writers in their classrooms. Jenkins, et al.'s (2009) description of a participatory culture is a helpful way of describing the specific features of what we mean when we talk about what a community of readers and writers in the classroom. We argue that incorporating RPGs into the ELA classroom is one way to create a participatory culture – a culture where students are encouraged to engage in imaginative and artistic work;

where students are supported and encouraged to create and share the texts they read and write, and where they feel connected to one another.

Although participatory cultures are most often found in the digitally-mediated worlds young people participate in outside of school, researchers have increasingly argued that meaningful learning can take place when participatory cultures are created within classrooms (Jenkins & Kelley, 2013). Indeed, although Gee (2007) refers specifically to the potential of videogames for learning, we believe that his arguments also extend to role-playing games. Role-playing games (RPGs) are games where players take on the identity of a single character in an imaginary world and try to solve problems and complete tasks with others over multiple sessions (Harrigan & Wardrip-Fruin, 2010). Within the narrative of the game, characters are able to grow, develop, and gain power over time (Harrigan & Wardrip-Fruin). There are a wide variety of types of RPGs including online versions, such as *World of Warcraft*, and tabletop versions, such as *Dungeon & Dragons*. In this chapter, we focus specifically on tabletop versions of RPGs. Although tabletop role-playing games are not digitally-mediated, they do meet many of the principles of good learning Gee sets out. We believe role-playing games are especially useful in the ELA classroom because of the ways in which they require problem-solving, foster imagination, and cultivate collaboration.

Although there has been extensive research on using computer games as tools for learning (Colby, & Colby, 2008; Egenfeldt-Nielsen, 2006), there are relatively few examples of using game-based learning in the ELA classroom or the effects game-based learning has on students' literacy practices (Steinkuehler, 2010). However, evidence suggests that simulations in which students take on a new role can have a significant effect on their writing ability (Troyka, 1974; Hillocks, 1986). Hillocks' meta-analysis of research on composition found that an environmental approach to instruction (such as when students have to inhabit a simulated role) led to improvements in students' writing. Specifically, Hillocks cited a study by Troyka (1974) who examined a control group and experimental group to teach writing. In the experimental group, students were presented with a "brief situation statement which gave the setting and background of the [rhetorical] problem as well as the action and rules for the simulation" (as cited in Hillocks, 1986, p. 124). The students were asked to work on these situation problems (i.e. a pollution problem, a neighborhood crime problem, a college campus drug problem, etc.) in groups. Each situation problem involved different writing strategies such as providing facts, describing incidents, and comparing and contrasting. An underlying assumption of the environmental approach to instruction is that engaging in these writing skills is complex and requires collaboration and feedback from others. This collaboration and feedback can be achieved through students interacting together as they work to solve various problems such as those implemented by Troyka (Hillocks, 1986).

Although Hillocks found Troyka's study compelling, he ultimately decided to leave it out of his meta-analysis of composition approaches because the significant effect size would skew the final results of his meta-analysis. Still, Hillocks (1986) argued that this study "should not be ignored" and encouraged researchers to further investigate the ways in which simulations can help students develop their writing skills. Although this chapter is not a research study, we do offer it as one example of what simulations, especially RPGs, can look like in the ELA classroom.

4 Narrative of Context

Elizabeth created this unit while enrolled in the English Education M.A.E.D. program at the College of William & Mary. She taught the unit during her 10-week student teaching internship in a sixth-grade English Language Arts class at a large middle school located in a suburban town in eastern Virginia. Elizabeth was an avid player of RPGs, and found many similarities between the imaginative worlds created in RPGs, and the imaginative world created when a reader becomes immersed in a novel. Elizabeth was also interested in providing opportunities for her students to connect their out-of-school literacy practices with in-school literacy practices. As she researched resources for her unit, she came across a dissertation study conducted by an English teacher, Kip Glazer, who had developed a model for using tabletop RPGs in the English classroom (2015). Because Glazer's model was based on sound, research-based pedagogical principles, and was clearly aligned with literature standards, Elizabeth felt comfortable adapting the model to her own classroom.

Elizabeth hoped that incorporating the RPG would better help her students grasp the ideas and concepts associated with the American Revolution. Oftentimes students have difficulty making meaningful connections to events that took place in the distant past. Thus, a primary goal of the Elizabeth's unit was to create a participatory culture where students could engage in collaborative discussions about their novels. Her hope was that through the game creation process students would deepen their understanding of key themes related to the American Revolution. A central aspect here was encouraging students to identify with the characters of their novels, and the conflicts those characters experienced. It was also important to highlight that just as the author of a novel crafts every element of the story (Glazer, 2015), so too would the students be crafting many elements of their RPG as they created characters and designed adventures. Thus, a secondary goal was that students would see themselves as creators, rather than just consumers, of texts. Elizabeth's unit included three main phases: book clubs, game creation, and game play, which we describe in more detail below.

5 Good Stories Make Good Games

Elizabeth started off the first day of the unit by asking students "What makes a good story?" The students were mostly in agreement in their answers. They said that a good story includes suspense, danger, romance, adventure, and so on. Elizabeth then asked, "What makes a game fun?" Here, students were much more divided on their answers. About half of the class thought winning was the most fun part of a game, while the other half did not think winning was necessary to have fun. Elizabeth then moved into a discussion of RPGs. Several students were familiar with popular tabletop RPGs like *Dungeons & Dragons* and *Pathfinder*, so Elizabeth was able to leverage the experiences these students had to help other classmates understand the concepts that go along with RPGs. After the discussion, Elizabeth provided students with a concrete definition of an RPG and explained its' discrete parts, "[An RPG is] an episodic and participatory story-creation system that includes a set of quantified rules that assist a group of players and a Game Master in determining how their fictional characters' spontaneous interactions are resolved" (Mackay, 2001, pp. 4–5). Elizabeth explained that the popular RPGs focus on compelling storytelling. The "participatory ... spontaneous reactions" of the players are what drives the direction of the story. The Game Master (GM) orchestrates the action of the story by setting up a scenario, and the players react. Elizabeth explained to her students that they would be crafting the development and progression of their story since they could decide how their characters would act and react to various scenarios.

For example, the GM could create an encounter where the players needed to retrieve plans from a British camp that would save countless Patriot soldier lives. The players then could make decisions for how they would complete this task. They could try and sneak into the camp undetected. Or they could throw caution to the wind and waltz into the camp demanding the plans be handed over. The story progresses based on the player's choices and because of this the possible outcomes and endings of story lines can vary wildly.

6 Book Clubs as Scaffolds for Participatory Game Creation

Just as RPGs have participants who play a variety of roles, so do book clubs. Each book club was made up of five to six students, each of whom had a specific role they would take on in the group. Elizabeth designed the book club roles from popular archetypes from RPG games. For example, the *Game Master* (GM) was in charge of leading the daily discussion and formulating discussion questions. The *Bard* sought out new and interesting vocabulary that would be unique to the context of the story. The *Scout* helped explicate and keep track of the settings discussed throughout the reading. Finally, the *Ranger* was tasked with finding passages worthy of close reading and further discussion.

To reinforce and scaffold the idea of roles within a collaborative context, each student was required to complete a role sheet each night for their reading assignment to ensure that there would be a fruitful discussion the next day in class. Oftentimes, the discussion between students developed organically because of the work they had put in the previous evening. For example, the *Game Master* might begin a discussion, and the *Ranger* would realize they had chosen a passage that fit well. The role sheets served to make collaborative discussion fluid and natural for the students.

Students worked in their book clubs for a week and a half. During this portion of the unit students were responsible for reading, discussing, and familiarizing themselves with the plot, characters and major themes in their respective novels. It was critical that the students had a deep understanding of their books because they were going to be responsible for creating a playable game that was set in the world of their novels. In order to effectively plan stories and create interesting characters, they needed to fully understand the context that those stories and characters lived in. After several days of discussion and reading, the students began to work on collaboratively constructing the RPG that was based on the world of their novels.

7 Writing Their Way into the Game: Game Master Guides, and Player's Handbooks

One defining feature of RPG's is the various resources available to players. In the game *Dungeons & Dragons*, for example, the *Dungeon's Guide* helps fledgling Game Masters understand how to create their own new worlds and how to craft compelling adventures. The *Player's Handbook* provides players an overview of the building blocks of creating new characters to play, such as their race (elf, dwarf, gnome) and class (ranger, wizard, fighter). Finally, Dungeon Masters can reference the *Monster Manual* when crafting encounters for the players.

These reference materials comprise the building blocks of an RPG. In Elizabeth's class, students were required to produce similar texts for their own RPG. Each group of students was responsible for creating the following texts: setting descriptions, game boards, novel character descriptions, created character descriptions, adventure scenarios and game rules. These were published on a website so that groups of students could see and play others group's games. Elizabeth created her own website prior to the unit that served as a model, or mentor text, for the students' websites.[1]

7.1 *Setting Descriptions*

RPGs rely heavily on a player's ability to imagine the fantastical world that surrounds their character. The Game Master helps facilitate full immersion by providing compelling and vivid descriptions of the world. In order to help the students begin to develop the world of their novel, each group member was required to select a major setting from their novel and write a short description incorporating language from the original text. Some students found writing solely in descriptive terms difficult. For example, Emily's first draft of her setting description of the prison in *Sophia's War* focused on describing why the setting was important to the story. Because the game creation required that players be able to vividly imagine the setting, Emily had to revise her writing to focus on the physical description of the British prison featured in *Sophia's War*. Her revised setting description set the ominous tone and mood for the prison setting that any Game Master could then use in their individual game sessions.

7.2 *Game Boards*

After the settings were selected and thoroughly described, each student created a physical game board based on their setting (see Figure 3.1). Emily's game board, for example, visually represent the tone and mood that she had created with her written description and included the prison structure as well as other features such as muddy roads, ditches, and pits full of refuse. The vivid description Emily had written, in conjunction with a visually accurate game board would serve as a scaffold to immerse her peers in the scenes of *Sophia's War*. Eventually, each novel had a number of different game boards at their disposal for all the major settings in their novels. When they began playing their sessions, these game boards were used to provide a visual support for where their characters were located relative to enemies, structures, and other features in the game.

FIGURE 3.1 A game board students created based on the novel *My Brother Sam is Dead*

7.3 *Character Creation*

One of the most important question RPG players can ask themselves as they play is, "Who am I in this world?" It is the player's responsibility to create a unique character, and then role-play that character throughout the game. In order to scaffold this new concept to the students, Elizabeth asked students to write a 150–200-word description of a major and minor character using quotes from the text. It was crucial that the students had a deep understanding of the different characters in the novel because these characters would likely play a part in the game sessions as NPC's (non-playable characters). The Game Master would need to have a thorough understanding of these characters so that when they were in the game they would respond appropriately.

7.4 *Adventure Scenarios*

Although RPG's are usually improvisational in regards to plot outcomes, there does need to be a skeleton of plot points in order to run a successful session. The adventure scenario assignment helped students develop these plot points for their games. The first part of the assignment was to create a polished "Adventure Trailer" that would be published on the students' website. This adventure trailer served as the advertisement for the scenario, and groups actually decided which adventure they wanted to play based on what they read in the trailer. The second part of the assignment was the preparation phase the GM would have to go through if the group decided to play through their session. The GM roughly sketched the various outcomes that could occur depending on the player's decisions and tried to anticipate the ways the players would have their characters behave. This portion of the assignment gave the students an idea of what types of responsibilities a Game Master has in an RPG. The assignment helped students understand that they were responsible for not only pitching their adventure, but also in charge of the specific details and game mechanics that would need to be considered while running a game session.

7.5 *Game Rules*

The final page on the students' website was dedicated to a list of rules the group created collaboratively. These rules had little to do with the mechanics of the actual RPG. Instead, they were agreed upon norms that the group would follow to encourage respect, teamwork, and communication. Some sample rules were, "The players will accept any ruling made by the Game Master" and "Players will come to an agreement before any major decision is made in the game". The game rules page was a way for the students to voice their expectations and desires regarding game sessions before anyone's feelings were hurt in the heat of the moment.

8 Playing the Game

Once the RPG was completed, and the students had a relatively firm grasp on the rules and mechanics, they were ready to learn the mechanics of playing an RPG. Teaching the students how to understand dice rolls, base values, modifier values and how to interpret them required a great deal scaffolding. The first step was to introduce students to a completed character sheet. Although RPGs are a font of possibility, these possibilities are tempered by a set of "quantified rules". All players have statistics or "stats" that show how proficient their characters are at certain skills. Elizabeth created a stat sheet for a character named Lisa Bennet to model how to develop the quantified rules (see Figure 3.2).

At first glance, the table (Figure 3.2) may look like a jumble of random numbers. But over the course of the unit students were able to not only interpret these character sheets, but also create them for their own characters. This character sheet ranks the proficiency a character has in four skills: Strength, Dexterity, Intelligence, and Charisma. To see the "ranking" you must look at their ascribed base value. The bottom table clearly shows the spectrum of the base values. 8 is the weakest while 14 is the strongest. Lisa's weakest skill is strength, base value of 8, while her strongest skill is charisma, base value of 14.

These base values are not just arbitrarily ascribed to Lisa. Within these four numbers hides her motivations, backstory and personality. Her low strength score demonstrates she is small girl thirteen years of age. Her higher dexterity

Character Name:	Lisa Bennett	
Health Points	20	
Skills	**Base Value**	**Modifier Value**
Strength	8	-1
Dexterity	12	+1
Intelligence	10	0
Charisma	14	+2
Weaponry or Items	**Damage or Effects**	
Revolver	1d4 + DEX Modifier	
Lock picks		

	Weakest			Strongest
Base Value	8	10	12	14
Modifier Value	-1	0	+1	+2

FIGURE 3.2 Elizabeth created a statistics sheet for a character named Lisa Bennett

and charisma skills represent her penchant for stealing and the quick wit she needed to survive after the British imprisoned her parents. The numbers must match the strengths and weaknesses to be effective in the game. When the students created their playable character they were also responsible for filling out a stat sheet that reflected the strengths and weaknesses of the character. In addition to modelling how to use the stat sheets, Elizabeth also modelled how an actual game session would be run using the fishbowl method. She created a scenario and acted as the GM while the students rotated in and out of game so that they could see the practical application of the abstract numbers they calculated. During the fishbowl, students experienced the ways in which the GM served as the driving narrative force during the game session. The GM drives the narrative by describing the setting, narrating the action, guiding the plot forward, and interpreting the dice rolls and rules.

We knew that students had engaged in a number of traditional literacies to get ready for their game play: they had read novels, written descriptive essays, and engaged in collaborative discussions. Finally, they were given three full class periods to explore the various settings and adventures their groups had created. As we watched the students play their games, we were struck by their affective responses to this pedagogical approach. Students laughed and talked as they rolled their dice, explored their worlds, and collaboratively created new adventures, challenges, and tasks for the characters they had created. As Aidan's comment at the beginning of our chapter indicated, being in the world of a book and actually making decisions as if one was a character in the time period is a completely absorbing experience. Games are, after all, a form of play – and as such are an immersive and enjoyable experience. As James, told us, "This was the coolest thing I've ever done in an English class".

9 Additional Resources

Elizabeth's website: Literaturecirclerpg.weebly.com

Interview with Elizabeth about her project: http://www.wmcild.org/2016/08/18/innovation-spotlight-elizabeth-deboeser-at-hornsby-middle-school/

10 Conclusion

In this chapter, we've argued that providing opportunities for young people to become immersed in the imaginative worlds of young adult literature through game creation emphasizes an aesthetic mode of reading (Rosenblatt, 1994/2005c). RPGs can provide students with opportunities to engage deeply with literature and write for a variety of purposes. Providing students with the opportunity to connect and extend their out-of-school literacy practices around gaming to traditional academic literacies helped create a participatory culture where students felt that their contributions – in the form of both talk and texts – mattered to those around them.

Note

1 See http://literaturecirclerpg.weebly.com/

References

Abrams, S. S. (2009). A gaming frame of mind: Digital contexts and academic implications. *Educational Media International, 46*(4), 335–347. https://doi.org/10.1080/09523980903387480

Anderson, L. H. (2008). *Chains*. New York, NY: Atheneum.

Avi. (2012). *Sophia's war: A tale of revolution*. New York, NY: Beach Lane.

Colby, R., & Colby, R. (2008). A pedagogy of play: Integrating computer games into the writing classroom. *Computers and Composition, 25*(3), 300–312.

Collier, J. L., & Collier, C. (1974). *My brother Sam is dead*. New York, NY: Four Winds.

Egenfeldt-Nielsen, S. (2006). Overview of research on the educational use of video games. *Digital Kompetanse, 3*(1), 184–213.

Gee, J. P. (2007). *What video games have to teach us about learning and literacy* (2nd ed.). New York, NY: Palgrave Macmillan.

Gerber, H. R., & Price, D. P. (2011). Twenty-first-century adolescents, writing, and new media: Meeting the challenge with game controllers and laptops. *The English Journal, 101*(2), 68–73.

Glazer, K. (2015). *Imagining a constructionist game-based pedagogical model: Using tabletop role-playing game creation to enhance literature education in high school English classes* (Doctoral Dissertation). ProQuest Dissertations Publishing. Retrieved from http://gradworks.umi.com/37/31/3731117

Harrigan, P., & Wardrip-Fruin, N. (2010). *Second person: Role-playing and story in games and playable media.* Cambridge, MA: MIT Press.

Hillocks, G. (1986). *Research on written composition: New directions for teaching.* Urbana, IL: National Conference on Research in English and Educational Resources Information Center.

Ito, M. (Ed.). (2010). *Hanging out, messing around, and geeking out: Kids living and learning with new media.* Cambridge, MA: MIT Press.

Jenkins, H., & Kelley, W. (Eds.). (2013). *Reading in a participatory culture: Remixing Moby-Dick in the English classroom.* New York, NY: Teachers College Press.

Jenkins, H., Purushotoma, R., Weigel, M., Clinton, K., & Robison, A J. (2009). *Confronting the challenges of a participatory culture: Media education for the 21st century.* Cambridge, MA: MIT Press.

Mackay, D. (2001). *The fantasy role-playing game.* Jefferson, NC: McFaland & Company.

Rosenblatt, L. (1994/2005c). The transactional theory of reading and writing. *Making meaning with texts* (pp. 1–37). Portsmouth, NH: Heinemann.

Steinkuehler, C. (2010). Video games and digital literacies. *Journal of Adolescent & Adult Literacy, 54*(1), 61–63.

Troyka, L. Q. (1974). *A study of the effect of simulation-gaming on expository prose competence of college remedial english composition students* (DAI 34: 4092-A. ED 090 541).

CHAPTER 4

Imparting Empathy with Gaming Experiences: A Conversation with the Developers of Thorny Games

Shelbie Witte and Jill Bindewald (with Oklahoma State University English Education Students)

1 Overarching Questions

1. In what ways does live action role playing (LARPing) align with your instructional goals?
2. How can LARPing assist in imparting empathy in a community of players (gamers, classmates)?
3. What insights does the epitext of Thorny Games impart a deeper understanding of the LARPing experience?

2 Introduction

Live action role playing (LARPing) became an educational tool (Edu-LARP) in 1916 when Inokentiy Nikolaevich Zhukov advocated for play in the classroom, arguing that children learn through imitation and self-education (Kot, 2012). LARPing is played in a chosen space, like outdoors or a classroom but is otherwise similar to the game *Dungeon & Dragons*. The grandmaster, the teacher in Edu-LARP, guides students through roles, either controlled or improvised, to optimize the learning experience (Kot, 2012). For example, a math class called the Hit Seekers was divided into music companies and assigned roles as artist, producer, and studio engineer and were each given one million dollars in play money to finance their projects. They acted their part through improvisation, which allowed them to learn about accounting and responsibility as they imitated these roles (Vanek 2017).

Little research exists about LARPing and learning. Brom, Dobrovolný, and Bromová (2015) suggest the reason that assessing LARPing and learning is difficult is that during the act of LARPing the participant is experiencing a different role. While in this state, the player's learning may not be assessed because the player is not acting as himself. To have the player switch to his own identity for assessment could disrupt the fluency of the game and learning.

 | DOI: 10.1163/9789004422315_006

However, a school in Denmark called Østerskov Efterskole uses EDU-LARPing as its curriculum. The school's standardized test scores remain at the national average overall and above average in some subjects (Gjedde, 2013; Hyltoft, 2012), suggesting LARPing is not harming (rather it may be improving) learning outcomes. Mochocki (2014) found in a pilot study that there is no significant difference between LARPers and traditional learners on standardized test scores. A consideration when examining data from standardized tests, is that Edu-LARP fits evidence-based rather than skills-based testing because students must often defend their actions to the grandmaster (i.e., the teacher) (Vanek & Peterson, 2016).

Though this limited evidence suggests that learning outcomes may remain the same for traditional students and LARPers, Mochocki's (2014) study revealed that students and teachers prefer the Edu-LARPing experience to more traditional educational experiences. Bowman and Standiford (2015) surveyed and interviewed middle school students who rated the LARPing approach high for learning preference and reported that it improved their attitudes towards science. Students were also motivated by narrative and the strategy when learning, which are key elements of LARPing.

Its enhancement of motivation to self-educate is the main reason researchers and educators advocate for LARPing in the classroom (Vanek, 2017; Vanek & Peterson, 2016; Bowman & Standiford, 2015). Vanek (2017) witnessed intrinsic motivation for learning when studying Ancient Mesopotamia with his students. Role playing as a priest, one student researched the salaries of clergy and constructed a compelling argument for higher pay. All the priests in his class were given higher pay for the student's well-articulated argument. In addition to demonstrating the students' motivation to learn more about their roles, researchers suggest LARPing reinforces emergent learning, problem solving, and empathy (Vanek, 2017; Bowman, 2010; Kot, 2012).

2.1 *LARPing in the Classroom*

In February of 2017, as part of the 21st Century Literacies Lecture Series hosted by the Initiative for 21st Century Literacies Research, the OSU English Education program was introduced to Thorny Games through the keynote speech of Dr. Antero Garcia, the keynote speaker for the event. Although we had heard of Live Action Role Playing experiences in the past, we hadn't considered the ways we could use LARPs in our own learning or in our future classrooms.

As teachers of writing, we understand the definition of writing to be broad to include the composition of thought in various modes, including the types of composition required to play LARPs. Each of us come from varied backgrounds in Oklahoma. Rural, suburban, and urban classroom experiences have each allowed us to better understand our roles as future teachers. Following the lecture, we spent our next *Teaching of Writing* course exploring Thorny Games, and playing Sign, one of three games introduced on the Thorny Games website. Our shared experience and reflection brought forward a set of questions for the game developers, Kathryn (Kate) Hymes and Hakan Seyalioglu, which we posed in a recorded Zoom interview.

OSU EE: Tell us how you both became game designers. What roads brought you together and then brought you to the work you're doing now?

Kathryn: Speaking for both of us, we became game designers out of a true love of games and out of being game players. We shared a passion for games as one of the basic axioms of our relationship starting from day one. Behind us, you can actually see our big library of board games.

Then after years of playing games and eventually becoming more involved in game communities, we were drawn into the story gaming community. The kind of games that are made within that community can be very deep and they don't shy away from difficult topics. Those games gave us amazing experiences that let us reflect on our lives in ways that other games hadn't. They dealt with story and empathy in a way that we hadn't experienced before.

There was the substance of games themselves, but also, there was the community that was built around it. It's a uniquely welcoming and encouraging community that values diverse voices. With that happy base to start from, we decided that we had to join in and be a part.

Hakan: We also saw certain stories that we wanted to tell and certain experiences that we wanted to help facilitate that we brought a unique perspective to. In particular with Kate's background in linguistics and my background in math and cryptography, we saw these as really rich topics to explore and wanted to help be a part of spreading awareness and love.

OSU EE: As adolescents, did you have favorite games to play that might influence your work now? Clearly the shelf behind you probably lends us to some interesting conversations about gaming. Tell us about when you were an adolescent, what made your heart sing? What really spoke to you?

Kathryn: This is a fantastic question.

Hakan: For me, it's a little difficult to say. I grew up in Istanbul in a pretty isolated environment. I never actually really had the community to really play the games that I was most interested in. I remember reading my first *Dungeons and Dragons* player guide in Turkish that I borrowed from my cousin and being fascinated by it, but I never had a group or a community that I could really play with. The games that I played as an adolescent were much more of the digital variety. I don't know that the games I most ended up playing were really reflective of what I wanted to play or not.

Kathryn: For me it's a digital game, *Myst*. I remember that being such a transformative experience. It was just so immersive, and I just remember getting so drawn into the story of this world and exploring it. I've always been drawn to world-building games and games that are heavily immersive since then. I think that has definitely been a theme of the kind of experiences we try to craft.

OSU EE: For Dr. Witte, who grew up in late 70's and early 80's playing Atari and going into Nintendo and Donkey Kong, she grew up along with video games. The first time she saw *Myst*, it was an immediate game changer.

Kathryn: What's so neat about *Myst* is it felt like it created a world and that you could continually reveal more detail as you got deeper into the story. The story and the world reinforcing one another is just a beautiful quality that still something that makes a game speak to me.

OSU EE: We are super curious about your design process. As future teachers, and as future teachers of writing, we think about writing process.

Kathryn: It can be chaotic at times since it's an extension of a complicated relationship and our own bonds together. I think that for us as designers, we often just start with who we are, what we want to say and what we are uniquely capable of saying. Ideas are so plentiful and they come so quickly, fast and furious. I still have notebooks where I'll jot down ideas. Sometimes I'll look back on them years later and it is just hysterical what struck you as being completely profound at some brief moment in the past.

Kathryn: Sometimes you'll find a particular idea that just seems to be the perfect nexus of what we can offer and that we really feel is important to put out into the world.The idea needs to be strong enough that we're willing to put in the time and effort to actually bring it to life. There are many things that you can slice and dice and say, hey, this may have a big audience or this might be financially successful but what's really important is "Are we really going to be able to put in the time and blood and sweat and tears in order to bring it out into the world?".

After going through that process, it usually means we have the core of an idea. Then it can depend. Sometimes we'll take an approach that starts with a game that already exists and seeing what would happen if you were just to map your idea to that design and then carve out, as you would a sculpture, parts that need to change in order to fit your original vision. That's one tactic.

Another is knowing a toolbox of mechanics and game design techniques holding each one up to the light and seeing if it is the right tool for what this idea calls for.

Hakan: The design process is really something that differs dramatically according to what stage you're in. I think very differently in the early stages of a game than I do in the last six months or so. And the last 10%, which is just as much important as anything else in the design, employs a drastically different skillset than the more abstract creative process.

Kathryn: In the beginning stages, the process is very internal. The ideas and trying to make something workable and playable is coming from us. Then you get to a point where you, because it's a game you're trying to craft and curate for other people, their input is the most important piece of the puzzle. We are huge practitioners of play testing. We prototype and playtest and have a whole worked regimen around it which has helped us go from first playable version to end stages.

OSU EE: We see so many similarities between your design process and what other artists use and what writers use and what musicians use, for example. You mentioned wanting to make a difference in the world and wanting to put something out in the world that makes a difference in some way. What is your inspiration to embark on the projects that you do? Would you say is it to make an impact in the world?

Hakan: I think there are a few perspectives on that. I think for our medium in particular, it's powerful if it's engaging and fun. It feels impossible to separate that from creating art in this medium. That has to be a partner in your ultimate vision.

On top of that though, we do see games as really such a core and important medium for imparting empathy and giving people grander perspectives on new topics. People don't really think a lot about language, despite being one of the most miraculous that we do as people. Just giving an appreciation for that and really letting people see a bit more of that magic in the world by itself is a big driver for us.

Kathryn: I think another part of what we do, and it really is about trying to put something good into the world, is actually spreading play just for the sake of play. There's so much value in being playful as adults. We are encultured to stop doing that at a certain age, and I feel like that's a very confining negative thing for a healthy well-rounded and optimistic life. You see baby animals, baby humans … Play just naturally bursts from them and it's only through these societal pressures and structures that adults stop doing it. Just spreading the value and preaching play is another element of what we make.

OSU EE: We love this idea of play for adults. You were right, as elementary age students are fairly uninhibited in their play and as they grow older they become self-conscious about how others perceive them and so those walls start going up. There's a lot of information out there about the idea that play and critical thinking have just been pushed to the side in our curriculum in middle school and high school. We are just really excited for the gaming insurgence, we are going to call it, where you can have fun and play but also build some critical thinking skills that have been pushed aside for so long, especially the players of the games that we've looked at that you've developed really have to think critically and analytically about what they're doing, at the same time they're enjoying it so much. We so appreciate that about the work that you've done.

Hakan: I think there are a couple different perspectives on that, too. There are a lot of games, especially digital games where a system is very strongly imposed on you and you're interacting with that system as is. Whereas for a lot of other systems like *Sign* I think we give you some scaffolding for an experience but really, it's what you put into it. Hopefully giving players that additional control and calling for their contribution and input is empowering.

OSU EE: What was the significance in the name Thorny Games?

Kathryn: Naming anything is a trial as I'm sure you know. We were looking at a number of options. We knew that our games were going to be pretty focused on language because we really see that as an extension of human stories. We also knew we would be exploring math and cryptography secrets – they're all just ways of looking at information more generally. We needed a name that at least fit one or two of those.

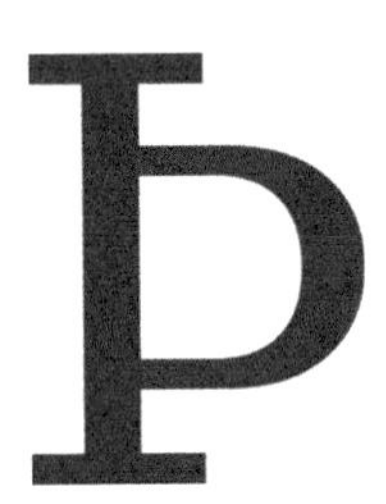

Thorn is a long lost letter that has a very interesting history in etymology. We wanted to draw on the history of language and bring that into just how we thought about our games. Also the symbol for thorn looks quite mathy – like a lot of variable symbols one would use. I think we had also just been to a Shakespeare festival and there was a quote from Hamlet ...

Hakan: The steep and thorny way to heaven.

Kathryn: We're like, oh, it all merges together and we had one of those -

OSU EE: Ah-ha moment.

Kathryn: Exactly.

OSU EE: The English teacher in each of us is geeking out. It didn't even occur to us that's what it was, but brilliant.

Kathryn: We've now weaved the thorn into our logo and a lot of other places.

OSU EE: Before we played *Sign* yesterday, we watched a YouTube video on Nicaragua and the Nicaraguan sign language. We needed to do that to build our background knowledge, to scaffold because most of us were starting from scratch. Isn't it beautiful that something like this can come from a real life experience that was had? Our minds were just blown that you have an inspiration like that that has evolved into *Sign*. As writers, we get an idea and sometimes what comes out at the end is something not at all related to what our initial inspiration was, but wow, we were just so impressed with what you did. How did you think to make the game Sign? We know the Nicaraguan sign language story plays into that, but how did you get from point A, sign language story, to B, *Sign*? Take us through how you got there.

Hakan: I think the story for that one is a surprisingly pragmatic one. There was a call for LARPs, a call for games at this game design challenge called the Golden Cobra which is a really wonderful annual game design challenge. Some of the prompts for that was touch was one and then the other one … Was it marginalized communities?

Kathryn: Unheard voices maybe. Or just looking for representation out of yourself.

Hakan: Both those prompts together reminded Kate of the story of Nicaraguan Sign Language.

Kathryn: That's a really important story for me in the fabric of humanity. I studied math and language in my academia period, and that is a story that is just so hopeful. It's a story about the birth of a modern language in the hands of children. Also children from a marginalized community in Latin America in the 70s which was a challenging and developing time.

When you think of typical stories in media from that era, they're usually about cartels, war and revolution. Amid all of that, there's this story that is just about the need to communicate and what comes out of children as they naturally play together. That thing was language. I think the story itself was so powerful that it was motivation to start carving it out into an actual experience.

How we actually got from that inspiration to the experience itself, it was using the same process that we talked about before. We've been players in this space for a while, so we have examples of other games that we've experienced and that really gave us fruitful inspiration for what works and what doesn't. Although, one thing that helped there was that we were fairly new players to LARP, or any kind of live action games, but we'd done enough that we were in this sweet spot where we were able to know some of the gross mechanics of what you need to take into account when a bunch of humans, but without being steeped enough in it to narrow your thinking. I find that that can happen sometimes when you're highly indexed in a community where begin to think just like the community. We were able to maintain our unique perspective while fitting it to the tools that we knew existed. Then it came down to getting something on paper, getting some feedback, and then finding some intrepid humans who would try it out.

Hakan: I think a lot of that also came from asking what the experiential thing we wanted the players to go through. What we had decided on was that we wanted to take players through this arc of not being understood and see what that means to them emotionally as they slowly gain tools for communication. Once we had that, the mechanics that we actually engaged then to make that happen, at least for *Sign* felt pretty clear.

Kathryn: I think that what is nice about *Sign*, too, and I definitely would love all of your feedback here, is that there's naturally some feeling of awkwardness or inhibition, not knowing what to do. In *Sign*, that feeling is entirely what you can imagine that child that you're embodying also felt on their first day of school. I don't know how to interact with people – I'm new.

The beginnings of the game, there's a lot of, I guess the term would be, bleed between what you are feeling as you, the player, and also probably what your character is feeling. That can be a really healthy way of processing those feelings and making them more approachable. You end up, as a player, having a really reinforcing experience with what your character is feeling.

OSU EE: We feel it is important for you to know that we have never had the type of experience that we had in class last night using *Sign*. We have tried various types of role play situations, various types of skits, various types of let's embody other people to try to help adolescents understand point-of-view of oppressed populations, to understand, to find empathy for, for example, how Jewish individuals must have felt in the Holocaust, to help students understand what the civil rights movement may have felt like. In every instance, these seem inappropriate. As future teachers, we feel like such phonies and posers for trying to recreate a situation in the classroom that just really can't be recreated, but in hopes of helping adolescents to have some empathy for the world. You guided us to do that in 15 minutes.

Kathryn: That's really sweet. I'm so glad.

OSU EE: We hope you understand what this can do for the classroom and for teachers. We cannot say enough about your vision and about the application of how it worked for us.

Kathryn: That's amazing to hear just because both of my parents were teachers with their whole careers in high school and middle school. I've always felt such kinship with that profession, but to know that we could contribute in that way is amazing.

Hakan: An observation that one player had of *Sign* is that one of the things that is surprisingly special about the game is that everyone else's main goal in it, as much as there is a goal, is to understand what you're saying, which really one of the fundamental things we all want from life. Actually, having that be somewhat of an organic goal in the game is something that's powerful and wasn't something we had really even thought of while writing it, but which has resonated with players.

OSU EE: We want to make sure we give space in the chapter to talk about *Dialect* and *Xenolanguage*. While *Sign* and *Dialect* have some real-world significance, what made you then divert in *Xenolanguage* to a science fiction type of LARP.

Kathryn: *Xenolanguage* is still very much in the alpha stages for us. I have long, long loved a set of stories by an author named Ted Chiang called *Story of Your Life*. This story ended up being both after we started thinking about *Xenolanguage* but before we finished it, released as the movie *Arrival*. I think a lot of people are now more familiar with that concept, but I think what's so neat about focusing on language is that for us it was really just a proxy for focusing on people more generally.

Putting that into a science fiction setting can give players a new freedom to broach subjects that are too close to home or that would be harder to embody in the world we live in. It gives people new freedom to really hunker down in different territory. One of our goals with that game is to see how science fiction allows us to better understand what it means to be human by contrasting it with something it isn't.

Hakan: Certainly all three games share some very core tenets and themes. Despite the fact that one's science fiction, they actually share a lot more than they diverge.

OSU EE: You talked about player reception and their feedback to you before. What kind of feedback are you getting along the way from the players that are playing. Clearly you have lots of positives, but also what are the some of the criticisms or critiques that have driven you to make changes?

Kathryn: That's a great question.

Hakan: I think some of the biggest pieces of criticism that we get from the games is that these games ask for a lot in terms of creativity and input from the players who may be used to more passive gaming experiences. Some of our games also can elicit very emotional responses which may not be something that everyone is expecting given their gaming experiences so far.

In a lot of ways, this is a very new field where expectations are set by adjacent communities. People may think they know all there is to know about roleplaying because they played a lot of *Dungeons and Dragons* or *Pathfinder*. You're totally welcome to and we think you'll have a great experience as long as you're going in expecting the right thing. But setting those expectations correctly is a very challenging thing when it's in a medium that people are already so attached to.

Kathryn: The other thing I call out here is feedback because it's something that we're actively seeking as this is a game about a community that we're not a part of. Deaf children are represented here and embodied, and we've gone through a very deliberate effort to try and get this right and it is a continually evolving process. Only through needing to print at one point will some definitive version be forced to exist in the world.

We've really tried to pack the right tools and framing and presentation in how the instructions are written so that it facilitates gameplay and lets players have an accurate experience with regard to the source material. One thing that we make a big point about in *Sign* is that it isn't meant to be an experience about what it is to be a modern deaf person.

Hakan: In terms of mistakes we've made and feedback that we've received, this wasn't something that was explicitly called out in early versions. This is something that we've gotten feedback on and that we took very seriously because we want to accurately represent what the game is, and isn't about. We're not going to get everything right all the time, and we hope to be solicitous and receptive to that feedback.

OSU EE: We recall your instructional manual is really helpful because you do specifically mention this is not to be a replay of modern deaf culture. Instead, you want players starting from a clean slate to be able to communicate with one another and trying to recreate that environment. That's different.

Hakan: Exactly.

Kathryn: It's very different.

Hakan: As one example, we learned something really important after talking to some members of the American Sign Language (ASL) community. Some people had some concerns at the very beginning that a lot of people have this really bad misconception about signed languages in general that they're not particularly expressive.

Neither of us realized that this was a preconception that people had – and if we present *Sign* as building something that resembles an actual signed language, then that's reinforcing that misconception. We took that very seriously and made changes to not reinforce that narrative.

OSU EE: To wrap up our conversation, what would be your message to someone who's picking up this book, a teacher or teacher educator, who likely has a little bit of interest in gaming but really hasn't used gaming as part of their curriculum. What would you say to those that have some interest in gaming but maybe haven't yet tried it? Why should they? What could we say to those that haven't yet but have the potential to do so?

Hakan: I think that the experiences that stick with us the most are conclusions that we draw ourselves. With our games, we're trying to make bigger points than the mechanics directly imply. At the end of the day, there's nothing mechanically empathetic about *Sign*. There's no empathy track that's going up. This is something that hopefully is emerging within the players themselves as they're playing.

Games I think offer a unique avenue in order to let students craft and build these experiences themselves, and hopefully that's the foundation for lifelong retention.

3 Conclusion

As teachers and future classroom teachers, we enjoyed being given the opportunity to meet with the gaming designers to discuss the design process and the thinking that supports the motivation of the gaming designers to put their work out into the gaming communities and classrooms. Our experience in playing *Sign* as learners and as future teachers helps us understand the impact LARPing can have on the motivation of students to become engaged in the topics more actively. Even more so, we hope to create classroom spaces that invite our students to create these types of learning experiences in order to advocate for a more active learning environment that embraces play and creative thinking.

References

Bowman, S. L. (2010). *The functions of role-playing games: How participants create community, solve problems and explore identity*. Jefferson, NC: McFarland.

Bowman, S. L., & Standiford, A. (2015). Educational larp in the middle school classroom: A mixed method case study. *International Journal of Role-Playing, 5*(1).

Brom, C., Dobrovolný, V., & Bromová, E. (2015). Towards in situ measurement of affective variables during playing educational LARPs: A pilot study. In R. Munkvold & L. Kolas (Eds.), *Proceedings of the 9th European Conference on Games Based Learning* (ECGBL 2015) (pp. 767–769). Nr Reading: Acad Conferences Ltd.

Gjedde, L. (2013). *Role game playing as a platform for creative and collaborative learning*. Reading: Academic Conferences International Limited.

Hyltoft, M. (2012). Full-time Edu-LARPers. In *Playing the learning game: A practical introduction to educational roleplaying based on the experiences from the LARP writer challenge* (pp. 20–23). Norway: Fantasi Forbundet.

Kot, Y. I. (2013). Educational larp: Topics for consideration. In *Wyrd Con companion book 2012* (pp. 118–127). Mountain View, CA: Wyrd Con.

Mochocki, M., 2014. Larping the past: Research report on high-school edu-Larp. In *Wyrd Con companion book 2014*. Los Angeles, CA: Wyrd Con.

Vanek, A. (2017). LARPs for learning. In M.Haiken (Ed.), *Gamify literacy* (pp. 25–43). Portland, OR: International Society for Technology in Education.

Vanek, A., & Peterson, A. (2016). Live Action Role-Playing (LARP): Insight into an underutilized educational tool. Learning, education and games. In K. Schrier Shaenfeld (Ed.), *Learning, Education, and Games: Volume Two: Bringing games into the educational context* (pp. 219–240). Pittsburg, PA: ETC Press.

PART 2

Videogames and Critical Literacies in ELA Classrooms

∵

Introduction to Part 2: Videogames and Critical Literacies in ELA Classrooms

Antero Garcia, Shelbie Witte and Jennifer S. Dail

Although the first half of this book focused on the specific approaches to instruction around gaming, the second half of this volume situates games and literacy practices within school structural and cultural contexts. We recognize that some of the barriers that hold back teachers from engaging in play-based pedagogies are not solely based on access, time, or a lack of ideas. Instead, there are substantial and lasting barriers to how teachers, students, schools, and society are shaped. By looking at several different aspects of this, we hope these chapters can help shift individuals' thinking as well as sustain school-based conversations about the possibilities of play.

We begin this section with Jon Ostenson's approach to unpacking representations of youth and adolescence within videogames. Building on the scholarship of Petrone, Sarigianides, and Lewis (2015), Ostenson both questions the role of adolescence and a developmental period and the effects of the label on individuals and representation. The chapter and the framework for analysis with students in classrooms is an important one for exploring various kinds of representation across the gaming landscape. For example, Ostenson asks students to explore, "How does the story told in this game reinforce and/or subvert the dominant constructs and perspectives we have about adolescents and this time of life?" These are empowering explorations that encourage youth agency and ownership around how narratives about broad swaths of people are understood. More importantly, we believe these are questions that can be broadened to look at representations of race, gender, class, and sexuality in games as well. Recognizing that games are plagued with "toxic" (Paul, 2018) cultural practices as represented by the Gamergate movement (e.g. Hurley, 2016; Quinn, 2017), it is important for students to explore how gaming systems both sustain and disrupt identities (e.g. Garcia, 2017).

Moving from broad social and cultural structures to the particular aspects of teacher development and learning, Glazer's chapter emphasizes ways that game creation can reflect models of teacher learning and proficiency. Echoing a similar call in our introduction to consider Shulman's (1987) call for kinds of pedagogical content knowledge, Glazer homes in on how making games can expand Technological Pedagogical and Content Knowledge (TPACK). This shift places several of the key ideas in this volume directly in conversation with

 | DOI: 10.1163/9789004422315_007

the research on teacher support, professional development, and evaluation. It speaks to important steps moving forward as a legitimate area of scholarship and teacher training.

Finally, we recognize that the notions of play – as something that college-educated, serious adults – should take part in is often seen skeptically. Further, the engrained models of learning shift adult thinking away from the imaginative, divergent thinking that is at the heart of how young people can play, dream, and design (e.g. Robinson, 2001). Sansing's chapter concludes this volume with a simple, direct exploration of why and how to play games and offers direct guidance for understanding play in case it has been a while since you've been deliberately engaging in playful activity for learning and pedagogy. From types of games to prompts for reflecting and making new multimodal artifacts, Sansing's chapter is a substantive list of ideas, actions, and ways to imagine. Embracing play across the field of education requires reimagining what happens in classrooms and we find it only fitting to conclude this volume with the activities and provocations of Sansing's chapter to get the proverbial ball rolling.

References

Garcia, A. (2017). Privilege, power, and Dungeons & Dragons: How systems shape racial and gender identities in tabletop role-playing games. *Mind, Culture, and Activity, 24*(3), 232–246.

Hurley, K. (2016). *The geek feminist revolution.* New York, NY: Tor Books.

Paul, C. A. (2018). *The toxic meritocracy of video games: Why gaming culture is the worst.* Minneapolis, MN: University of Minnesota Press.

Petrone, R., Sarigianides, S. T., & Lewis, M. A. (2015). The youth lens: Analyzing adolescence/ts in literary texts. *Journal of Literacy Research, 46*(4), 506–533.

Quinn, Z. (2017). *Crash override: How Gamergate (nearly) destroyed my life and how we can win the fight against online hate.* New York, NY: Public Affairs.

Robinson, K. (2001). *Out of our minds: Learning to be creative.* West Sussex: Capstone.

Shulman, L. S. (1987). Knowledge and teaching: Foundations of the new reform. *Harvard Educational Review, 57*(1), 1–23.

CHAPTER 5

A Critical Examination of Adolescence through Video Games

Jon Ostenson

1 Overarching Questions

1. How does the fact that adults generally create videogames with teenage characters potentially shape the portrayal of teenagers in these games?
2. How might videogames featuring teens or adolescent situations reinforce or challenge the portrayals of teenagers in other popular media?
3. Videogames are often praised for being interactive, but how do the inherent limits of a player's agency in games with teen characters serve as commentary on the restrictions placed on teenagers in broader society?
4. How might adult players be influenced by the representations of teenagers they encounter in games with teenage characters?
5. What might be the appeal of these games to adult players?

2 Introduction

There are many ways we can bring the serious study of videogames into a classroom. The most obvious might revolve around these games' capacity for storytelling, with connections to be made to traditional activities of literary interpretation or creative writing. In this approach, we consider a videogame as a textual object, which focuses our attention on specific features of the game and the player's experience with the game.

In a framework for exploring literacy and videogames outlined by Australian researchers (Apperly & Beavis, 2013; Beavis, 2014; Beavis, Apperly, Bradford, O'Mara, & Walsh, 2009), this is one of two perspectives we could take. They suggest that focusing on games as text includes a focus on the narrative aspects of games but also critical perspectives on games and how issues of identity and ideology may be brought out in the relationship between the game and the players. This is the focus of this chapter, where I make a case for looking at videogames with teenage characters as a manifestation of the cultural construct of adolescence.

 | DOI: 10.1163/9789004422315_008

3 Theoretical Framework

As an English teacher, one of the attractions of videogames is as a storytelling medium. Stories, however, do not exist independently of the culture in which they're formed and shared. They often mirror the preoccupations of a culture, and the themes of these stories can shed light on culturally embedded ideologies. A primary project of the discipline of English can be to explore and uncover these subtle but nonetheless recognizable embedded ideologies in the stories that surround and influence us. And videogames with heavy storytelling elements can certainly fit the definition of culturally influential stories, especially where adolescents (a target audience for video games) are concerned.

One deeply embedded cultural idea that can be of interest to young players is adolescence as a developmental category. Several modern, notable videogames feature teenaged protagonists and settings and conflicts that are familiar to adolescents, and portrayals in these games are arguably reflective of embedded cultural ideas. Youth studies scholar Nancy Lesko (1996, 2012) explains that traditional ideas about this age group are often bounded by biological factors, resulting in seeing teens as driven primarily by out-of-balance hormones and other physical disruptions brought on by puberty, swayed in irrational directions by an overweening peer influence, and generally deficient when compared to adults. Such notions, she argues, are not inevitable but rather are imposed to a great degree on adolescents by the constructions that adults have made due to historical and political forces that have projected society's fears about race, gender, and social progress onto this age group; this, in turn, has defined them as needing protection and shepherding if we are to have confidence in their future and that of society.

Another scholarly movement seeks to examine the potential of stories written for and about adolescents to propagate and disrupt these cultural ideas through the use of a Youth Lens to interpret literature (Petrone, Sarigianides, & Lewis, 2015). Although these writers have focused attention on print books written for teens, I suggest here that videogames offer another storytelling medium rich with opportunities for critical investigation. As a form of literary criticism, a Youth Lens works from the implications of the construction of adolescence (and the incipient deficit views of adolescents) and investigates how portrayals of adolescents and their lives are "part of cultural discourses of adolescence/ts that carry larger ideological messages" (Petrone et al., 2015, p. 511). Since these stories (including those in videogames) may be written *by* adults *for* adolescents, we can see this medium as ideological, where the adult author's norms are communicated to the younger reader in a manner designed to exercise power or influence (Nikolajeva, 2010). A recognition of this power dynamic can empower young readers to "recognize and critique the adult norms and goals anchoring" stories written for them (Petrone et al., 2015, p. 512). As a former high school English teacher and in my position today at the university, this is the enterprise that most interests me and that has influenced the activities that I describe here.

4 Providing a Lens

To help students see the way these cultural ideas work as described here, we first need to make them aware of the way that our ideas about adolescence transcend the biological and enter the realm of a cultural construct with its own set of expectations. I initiate this process by asking my students to brainstorm a list of characteristics they associate with teenagers; this activity consistently generates a list of fairly negative ideas about what is often seen as an angst-ridden, disrupted, and confusing stage of life. I then ask my students to reflect on their own teenage years and share how accurately they think the list describes their experience. Students often take issue with some of the descriptors they just associated with the teenager; when pressed, they readily acknowledge that they were thinking of a "typical" teen and not necessarily their own selves.

This leads us to the first important recognition: there is an ideal (a construct) that exists outside of their own experience that defines the typical adolescent. When I ask where they think this construct has come from, they often share experiences with older siblings, overheard conversations with adults, and even their observations of peers. We identify media and stories aimed at teenagers as a major contributor to this construct. To further develop their understanding of the cultural construct and its influence, students explore specific instances, primarily TV shows and movies, that feature teenagers as main characters, in familiar settings (schools, parties, part-time employment), and with recognizable themes (discovering one's self, navigating teen-adult relationships, losing one's innocence). They view these media and stories outside of class, observe how the construct is being reinforced or challenged, and report their findings back in the classroom. Throughout this process, we talk about how these representations not only reinforce common deficit views of teenagers but how they also serve to privilege and proselyte for (often quite subtly but at times in heavy-handed ways) adult norms of behavior, what we tend to consider as "mature".

With this recognition more firmly established, I introduce students to the two guiding questions that, in line with suggestions from Petrone et al. (2015, p. 511), should guide our critique of these constructs in video games:

1. How does the game portray adolescents or the period of time we call adolescence?
2. How does the story told in this game reinforce and/or subvert the dominant constructs and perspectives we have about adolescents and this time of life?

In general, I ask students to focus on the typical elements of storytelling as evidence for the answers they provide to these questions. We can focus attention, logically, on characters and their behaviors and actions in videogames, but we can also look at settings and plot events and general themes in our quest to understand the way a cultural construct of adolescence informs the way these games are written and experienced.

Although videogames are often targeted at teenaged audience, there isn't a long tradition in videogames of including teen characters or storylines that are directly connected to teens' lives. This has started to change recently, with a handful of recent games focusing their storylines on a teenage world. In this next section I focus on the story-driven game *Oxenfree*, from Night School Studio, as an example of how we can turn this critical lens on a videogame.

5 Case Study: *Oxenfree*

Oxenfree is a supernatural thriller, with isolated, creepy settings and haunting encounters with disembodied spirits. The story involves five high school juniors who head out to Edward's Island for an evening beach party. While there, they stumble upon supernatural forces found through tuning a handheld radio to specific frequencies, launching the player into the middle of a supernatural mystery. The player takes on the role of a teenager named Alex, and much of our time as a player is wrapped up in conversations, where dialogue options appear around Alex's head. In *Oxenfree*'s most unique feature, however, these options do not wait patiently for us to consider them, as in other games with a dialogue-heavy focus; instead, they fade rather quickly if no choice is made. The plot itself unfolds through the player's actions, which take place in a 2D/3D world that's a mix of traditional, point-and-click adventure games and platform games. The radio serves as the primary device for building puzzles into the game which, although rather simple in nature, help us piece together the story behind the supernatural events.

In general, this game can be analyzed through a Youth Lens by focusing on the small set of characters in interaction with each other, on design choices made by the game's developers, and on some dramatic moments that occur throughout the game's narrative arc. By using the primary analytic questions mentioned above (and variations on these questions tailored to examine literary elements), we can use this game as an example of how a critical lens can be applied to such a text and guide students through a meaningful analysis of the embedded constructs of adolescence.

5.1 *Characters or Caricatures?*

In the opening scenes on a ferry to Edward Island and subsequently on the island's beach, we are introduced to the five characters in the game: Alex, our hero, who recently lost her brother, Michael (who, although dead, maintains a presence as strong as a physical character); Jonas, whose mother is marrying Alex's father thus making him her step-brother; Ren, a boy who's been Alex's friend for a long time and seems unsettled by the abrupt appearance of Jonas in her life; Clarissa, a popular girl who dated Michael before he died; and Nona, a quiet girl who mimics Clarissa caustic attitude when they're together, but demonstrates a more independent, gentle character on her own. In many ways, these characters represent traditional types that are often portrayed in stories about and for teenagers: Ren is something of a stoner and spends his time playing guitar and videogames; Clarissa is cast as a typical "mean girl" and Nona is a clingy groupie who's struggling to find her own sense of self outside of Clarissa's shadow. Even the setting for our introduction is familiar: an illicit overnight beach party that's part of a tradition at the local high school, involving drinking and typical party games like Truth or Dare (called Truth or Slap in the game).

Students can explore how these early characterizations reinforce (and are reinforced by) the cultural constructs of adolescents. Why choose to show these dimensions of these characters? What do the types represented by these characters reveal about how adults construct teens' identities? Students can also be on the lookout while playing the game for clichés that tap into these constructs, such as when it becomes apparent that Ren is jealous of the role that Jonas is playing in Alex's life–while this is not an explicit love triangle, such an arrangement is not uncommon in stories for teenagers, and students can question why adults incorporate this trope so frequently into stories for and about teens.

These are early introductions, however, and as the game progresses, these characters unfold. As students progress through the game, they should be encouraged to consider how the developers provide additional dimension to these characters and flesh out their personalities. In what ways do these additional encounters reinforce typical representations of youth (as in Ren's jealousy of Jonas, for instance) and in what ways do they challenge these (as in the way the developers suggest we feel more sympathy for Clarissa or Nona, who have both suffered tragedies that may shape their current relationships with other characters). As we gain insights into these characters, thanks to the developers' selective revelations, we can ask critical questions about why some traits of teenagers seem to be reinforced and why we're encouraged to see others in more nuanced ways.

5.2 *Teens and Risky Behavior*

Early in a story-driven game, players must experience an inciting incident, similar to what we'd find in any print story. This incident comes in *Oxenfree* after the beach scene described above, when Ren leads Alex and Jonas into a cave near the beach. In this cave, he demonstrates how the radio can be tuned to receive broadcast signals while standing by cairns of stacked rocks; one of these signals sets off a light in a deeper part of the cave that Jonas and Alex decide to explore, beginning a chain of events that launches the game's central mystery. Ren stays behind to eat a "magic brownie" (laced with marijuana), which ends up being a bit too strong for him and casts doubts on his ability to help later in the game.

A discussion of these opening moments through the Youth Lens would begin by asking students to consider how adults tend to view teens' behaviors as risky; students I've worked with in the past would suggest that adults see teens as impulsive, lacking the kind of judgement and appreciate for consequences that are part of "normal" adult behavior. They often mention the fact that insurance rates for drivers drop precipitously at age 25, once that famed frontal cortex is developed. They also talk about how teenage years are often seen by adults (and teens, perhaps because they think it's expected of them) as experimental years, where teens try on different behaviors and personas as part of a quest for identity. We can talk as a class about how these views often contribute to adults' perceptions of teens as deficient.

Students can then turn their attention to the design choices made in the early moments of this game. Tapping into their experience with the genre, we can ask students about how designers usually provide a justification for the player's character to take risks or engage in dangerous behavior. Often the player is cast in a specific role (such as that of adventurous archeologist in the Lara Croft games or an elite soldier in the Call of Duty series); other times a more emotional motivation might be employed (an otherwise normal man goes to extremes for revenge, as in the Max Payne or Grand Theft Auto games).

We might ask students to find the significance in the fact that none of the characters in *Oxenfree* have any kind of background like this. These characters are presented simply as teenagers, and no other motivation for their behavior is given than that they want to have fun. Risk plays a central role early in the story: the teens are on the last ferry to the island, stranding them all night on the island; to get to the beach, players must climb on top of a dumpster and scale a fence designed to keep them off the beach. We can ask students if, in these choices, the designers (all of whom, we should remember, are adults) perpetuate the construct of teens as impulsive, risk-taking young people who give little thought about future consequences? How do they leverage this construct in building the game and compelling the player forward into the action? Do they do anything to subvert this construct?

Of interest in these scenes is that the behavior of Jonas and Alex, in exploring the unknown cave, is juxtaposed with Ren's use of drugs–a choice that is revisited later in the game as a potential hindrance during a puzzle sequence. One way of seeing this juxtaposition is as a way of passing judgment on Ren, who incapacitates himself in a way by consuming the brownies (and can be judged harshly for this by Alex if the player so desires); in contrast, the risks that Jonas and Alex continue to take throughout the game help move its action forward to a resolution and are thus seen more positively. Risks in videogames are often rewarded, being part of the fabric of games in general, but *Oxenfree* allows us to ask questions about how teenagers and adults generally view risks for this age group, and how those views are reinforced by social constructs.

5.3 *Agency and Dialogue*

Any discussion of the construct of adolescence and the deficit views of adults that emerge from this construct must touch on teenagers and agency. What power is denied teens thanks to these dominant deficit views of their age group? How do narratives that build on this construct explore teenagers' choices and use of power? How do they position teenagers as capable or incapable? How does the setting in which these stories take place reinforce teens' agency or detract from it? These questions can all be used to great effect as students play and analyze *Oxenfree*.

In a move that isn't atypical for stories told about teens, adults are not physically present in this game, thus requiring the teen characters to fend for themselves. One connection to the normal, adult world are the radios scattered across the island which represent a possible hope for rescue but which are consistently found broken and useless. Students should be encouraged to explore what this design choice suggests about the developers' perspectives on teens and their ability to fend for themselves. Additionally, students can be asked to consider which characters in the game take the initiative and act, and which characters are seen more as objects. For instance, in the inciting incident in the cave, it's Jonas who first explores the cave, almost forcing Alex's (and the player's) hand in initiating the game's central action. At other crucial decision points in the game (such as when players decide whether to find Ren or Clarissa), others might make suggestions, but all is still subject to Alex's agency (and, by transference, the player's). In particularly important moments, the other characters become possessed by the spirits that haunt the island, and they lose all agency until Alex (using the radio) can free them. What is the connection in all these events between the designers' conceptions of teen capacity and Alex's ability to choose? Do these portrayals reinforce or challenge traditional constructs that might cast teens in powerless situations? With *Oxenfree*, students can consider how casting a teenager as the hero challenges constructs of adolescence and what is suggested by having some characters (such as Ren or Clarissa) play less active roles.

The notion of agency is particularly explicit in the player's most frequent choices, in the form of the dialogue bubbles that frequently appear around Alex's head. These choices allow the player to shape Alex's identity, in a sense, if they choose an option based on the tone it suggests. As with all videogames, our control of a virtual person in terms of the game raises interesting questions about agency, but in the case of a teen character, some students might be interested in discussing how Alex could be a metaphor for teens who feel their agency is thwarted by outside forces seeking to control them or shape their identities. This might also be related to the moments when characters are possessed, and we could productively explore how this might relate to fears about teenagers being "controlled" by peers or the media. Other students might be interested in exploring the atypical option given in this game to avoid conversation at all. What might a silent Alex suggest about cultural views of teen's voices or how our voice is often connected to our power over the world around us?

Choice and control are fundamental to videogames, and most players are unlikely to be drawn to a game that offers little of either. But in the context of teenage characters in videogames, the ability to choose and exercise control over the environment can take on new dimensions related to cultural constructs of adolescents.

6 Conclusion

This case study represents only one example (and I have selected only a few possibilities from many that surface in *Oxenfree*) for applying a critical lens to the study of videogames. As these games continue to permeate the lives of adolescents, it makes sense for teachers to help guide them in thinking critically about how these games reinforce or challenge cultural narratives and constructs about being a teenager or becoming an adult. While many might see the primary purpose of videogames to be entertainment (and they certainly deserve that label), we see today more and more games that seek to entertain in the same way that great literary works entertain: through thought-provoking portrayals of that which we think we already understand that encourage us to reconsider our views of others and the world around us. For young people who find themselves in the stage of life we've labeled as adolescence, examining portrayals like those in *Oxenfree* and other games can help them become more sensitive to the ways that cultural norms and expectations are reinforced and communicated, and the ways that we might question them.

References

Apperly, T., & Beavis, C. (2013). A model for critical games literacy. *E-Learning and Digital Media, 10*(1), 1–12.

Beavis, C. (2014). Games as text, games as action: Video games in the English classroom. *Journal of Adolescent & Adult Literacy, 57*(6), 433–439.

Beavis, C., Apperly, T., Bradford, C., O'Mara, J., & Walsh, C. (2009). Literacy in the digital age: Learning from computer games. *English in Education, 43*(2), 162–174.

Lesko, N. (1996). Denaturalizing adolescence: The politics of contemporary representations. *Youth & Society, 28*(2), 139–161.

Lesko, N. (2012). *Act your age: A cultural construction of adolescence*. New York, NY: Routledge.

Nikolajeva, M. (2010). *Power, voice and subjectivity in literature for young readers*. New York, NY: Routledge.

Petrone, R., Sarigianides, S. T., & Lewis, M. A. (2015). The youth lens: Anlayzing adolescence/ts in literary texts. *Journal of Literacy Research, 46*(4), 506–533.

CHAPTER 6

Video Game Creation as an Instructional Strategy: A New Way to Apply the TPACK Framework in K-12 Education

Kip Glazer

1 Overarching Questions

1. What are the benefits of allowing students to create videogames?
2. What are the practical instructional processes to incorporating game-creation?
3. What tools and resources will classroom teacher need to make this a successful instructional practice?
4. How does the TPACK Framework apply to this instructional strategy?

2 Introduction

As a former high school teacher and instructional technologies coach, I have heard from many teachers about the difficulties of incorporating instructional technologies into their instructional days. Many of them understand and agree that instructional technologies are not only preferable but also essential in today's learning environment. However, teachers often express concerns, even fears, of not being able to use them effectively. Furthermore, when I shared my research on incorporating gaming into classroom instruction, I have seen their worry turning into a full-blown panic. Teachers often said that they did not have the time to create the games for their students to use. Having been a classroom teacher for over a decade, I completely understand and agree with their concerns.

In this chapter, I will describe how I scaffolded the students' learning process with *Construct 2*[1] as a way to incorporate gaming into my classroom practice. Using the principles of Design-Based Research method (Barab, 2006; Barab & Squire, 2004; Van der Akker, 2000), this chapter will describe the first iteration and lessons learned as a springboard for future iterations.

 | DOI: 10.1163/9789004422315_009

3 Statement of the Problem

Whenever I heard such concerns described above from teachers, I asked them to think back to their first teaching experience. I challenged them to consider how much they learned by preparing the instructional materials to teach their students. I encouraged them to reflect on how they had to read and process the information that they acquired through reading to create effective lesson plans. Then I transitioned to discussing game creation by students as an instructional strategy.

Rather than take on the responsibility of creating the games for their students to use, teachers should leverage the game creation, in particular, videogame creation, in high school classrooms as a serious instructional strategy for their students to learn vital literacy, numeracy, computational, and artistic skills. When students create and teach others, they are learning more than simply playing games created by others.

4 Why Game-Based Learning

Over the years, scholars have consistently argued the benefits of using videogames in the classroom for learning. According to Gee (2013), well-designed video or digital games require players to actively participate in an interest-driven learning process through tackling carefully sequenced challenges. Therefore, video or digital games are one of the most effective learning tools for the modern society. Because games allow students to experience sophisticated modeling, students can create mental models and move beyond simple knowledge acquisition (Squire, 2011). In his study on the player behaviors of *World of Warcraft* (WOW), a massively multiplayer online role-playing game (MMORPG), Chen (2012) argued that while playing well-designed video or digital games, learners gained opportunities to produce, consume, remix, and critique all sort of media. Gameplay provided the game players with multiple opportunities to communicate, collaborate, problem solve, and even metacognate, making it an ideal tool for learning (Chen, 2012).

Bogost (2007) extended Gee's argument to what he called "procedural rhetoric" (p. 1) as he espoused the benefits of videogames. He argued that the power of videogames resided in their complex *rhetoric* that provided adaptive yet persuasive responses based on the players' actions and reactions during gameplay. In other words, videogames allowed players to connect specific experiences with specific content by moving them through a systemic process similar to a persuasive speech (Bogost, 2008). According to Bogost (2007), playing videogames forced players to examine their biases as videogames did not allow players to remain passive consumers of another persons' creation. He further emphasized that videogames offered sophisticated and fully developed authoring experiences for the player beyond a simple combination of verbal, written, and visual rhetorics typical of conventional multi-media such as movies or videos.

In today's media-saturated society where most students are accustomed to actively participating in the knowledge creation utilizing various social media platforms, a conventional pedagogy that focuses on a linear progression is grossly inadequate in preparing students for the future (Gee, 2003, 2004). Concerned scholars and educators have worked to correct such issues by arguing for the use of digital games and computer simulations in the classroom to improve student motivation and engagement. Gee (2013) argued that the use of videogames and computer simulations in the classroom allowed students opportunities to think deeper about the materials they are learning since humans think and understand best when they can fully engage their imagination through play.

Furthermore, well-designed videogames require players to actively participate in an interest-driven learning process through tackling carefully sequenced challenges, making it one of the most effective learning tools for modern society (Gee, 2013). Squire (2003) identified two ways that videogames have been used in education. First, games have been used to train a specific set of skills or to provide information (Jonassen as cited in Squire, 2003; Sitzmann, 2011). Second, games have simulated highly dangerous and often costly real-life situations for consistent training of the users, including pilots or other military personnel. Low-fidelity simulations and strategy games have also been used to develop skills such as manipulation of variables, development of varying perspectives, abilities to simulate hypothetical events, visualization of dimensions, and comparison of simulations (Squire, 2003).

To prepare for a more globally networked society of today where access and the ability to gain such access to information have become imperative for success, students must be given learning opportunities to become producers of new knowledge (Benkler, 2006; Black, 2008; Jenkins, 2006). Because games allow students to experience sophisticated modeling, students can create mental models beyond simple knowledge acquisition (Squire, 2011).

4.1 *Videogame Creation as a Way to Develop New Kind of* TPACK *in K-12 Education*

However, playing the game only allows the players to temporarily reside in the game creator's imaginary world. Teachers need an instructional strategy that maximizes their students' learning in a new teaching environment steeped in instructional technologies. Using their pedagogical expertise, teachers must be able to use technology to teach their content, and the Technological Pedagogical and Content Knowledge (TPACK) framework addresses the needs for seamless integration of three major elements (Koehler & Mishra, 2009).

The TPACK model (also known as the TPCK) traces its origin to Shulman's (1987) *Pedagogical Content Knowledge* (PCK), a paradigm for researching teacher effectiveness. Mishra and Koehler (2006) expanded Shulman's ideas to include technological knowledge in their new, expanded framework known as the Technological Pedagogical and Content Knowledge framework (TPACK) (see Figure 6.1). Mishra and Koehler (2006) built a flexible framework that could both inform and evaluate the effective teaching practices as more and more teachers began to incorporate technology into their daily teaching practices. With the addition of technological knowledge into the framework, TPACK provided a useful framework that represented the complexity of teaching in today's classroom (Chai, Koh, & Tsai, 2013). Rather than restricting the players to stay in the purview of the game creator, teachers can leverage videogame creation to encourage their students to interact with both the technology and the content in a meaningful fashion.

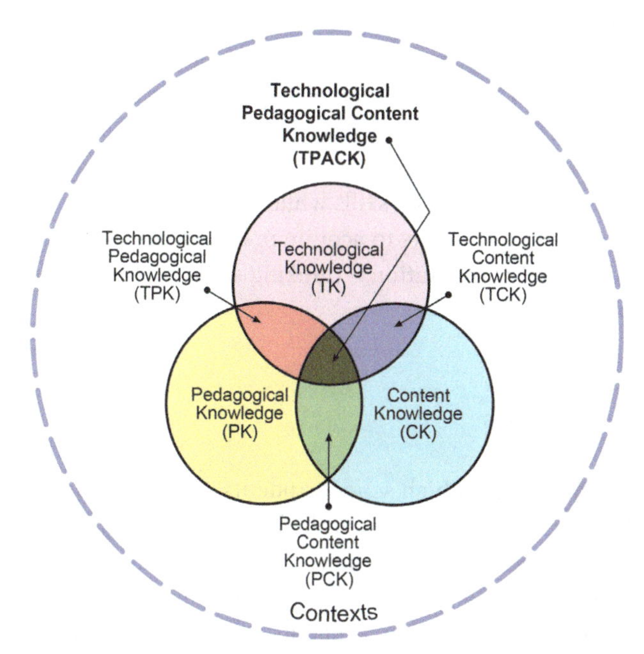

FIGURE 6.1 The TPACK image (http://tpack.org, reproduced by permission of the publisher, © 2012 tpack.org)

Based on the understanding that students learn better creating in a situated environment through collaboration (Brown, Collins, & Duguid, 1998; Brown, Collin, & Newman, 1989; Greeno, 2006; Martin & Stager, 2013), I argue that video game creation is a superior solution to simply playing a game due to its ability to effectively facilitate the transformation of the learners into knowledge producers (Benkler, 2006; Black, 2008; Gee, 2003; Jenkins, 2006). Because the students must actively participate in the creation process, videogame creation naturally allows students to become true co-creators of the knowledge (Kafai, 2009; Papert & Harel, 1991).

Game creation, therefore, embraces the central tenants of the TPACK framework since it naturally allows the students to use education technology to interact with the content as the teacher guides them to become competent learners and game creators. As they create videogames, students are able to take advantage of the teachers' TPACK. Game creation resides in the space where technology, content, and pedagogy seamlessly interact to elevate student learning (Koehler & Mishra, 2009).

4.2 *Narrative of Context*

To move students from acquiring basic *literacy skills* to more complex *literary skills,* teachers must implement instructional strategies that can lead to authentic assessments. Such transition is possible when teachers allow students to research how to use videogame making tools, encourage them to share their knowledge by teaching each other, and then instruct them to create the final product that demonstrates their deep understanding. Because videogame creation is a multi-layered learning activity, students can practice their reading, writing, listening, and additional artistic skills while creating their games. Furthermore, it allows high school students to acquire practical skills such as computer coding and additional computational thinking skills, making it an ideal instructional strategy.

5 Lesson Steps and Examples

In the 2014–2015 school year, eighteen high school students at a comprehensive high school in California's Central Valley enrolled in a web-design class created two videogames using *Construct 2*. The class consisted of students from all grade levels with three female and fifteen male students, and all students elected to take the class. Although none of the students knew how to create a videogame using *Construct 2* at the beginning of the semester, they were able to create a simple game on their own first, and then created more complex games in pairs. The process was designed to help the students gain technological competency as well as content knowledge, in particular math and science.

First, I introduced the tool. During this phase, students were instructed to interact in an online class forum known as *Haikulearning* to share the information that they gathered about the video-making tool. I chose this tool because it had a robust discussion board, which allowed them to collaborate continuously. After being introduced to the video-making tool, students were instructed to begin a threaded discussion about what they discovered by researching the tool. They listed the top ten YouTube tutorials, useful online forums, and blogs on the discussion board. Each student was responsible for creating one forum post and explaining why the resources that they found were superior to other resources. Students were also required to read at least three forum posts and comment on them. They were also asked to evaluate at least one full online thread that included several posts. Students used a rubric that included categories such as quality, validity, and usefulness of the resources. They also evaluated each other's resources and created a video tutorial to demonstrate their knowledge. The video tutorial had to include at least one useful feature of *Construct 2*. Prior to recording their tutorials, students were asked to write scripts and create presentations using Google Slides for the video. Once again, each student had to evaluate at least one other presentation and the attached script. For this assignment, students used a rubric with categories such as logical flow, quality of screenshots, and usefulness of the chosen feature. Students learned to research and evaluate the information and then present it in a coherent manner.

At this point, my focus was for the students to simply learn to use the tool rather than getting them to produce high-quality videogames. This step served two purposes. First, by researching and watching various tutorials, they were becoming familiar with how to use the tool. Second, students were able to articulate why a certain resource was better than the other, which demonstrated their analytical and evaluative skills.

Once the students learned how to use the tool, they created their first simple game independently. While researching, students discovered that the *Construct 2* website also featured various games that could be used as a template. Seeing the examples, the majority of the class opted to create 2-D games that had a simple figure moving from left to right or top to bottom on the screen while attempting to capture stationary objects. Few opted to create original games because they knew what was possible after seeing several tutorial videos (see Figure 6.2). In the end, all of the students were able to create simple games. While completing their first game, students were required to create a planning document and a learning log that contained what they learned each

FIGURE 6.2 A screenshot of a student-created game called *Void*

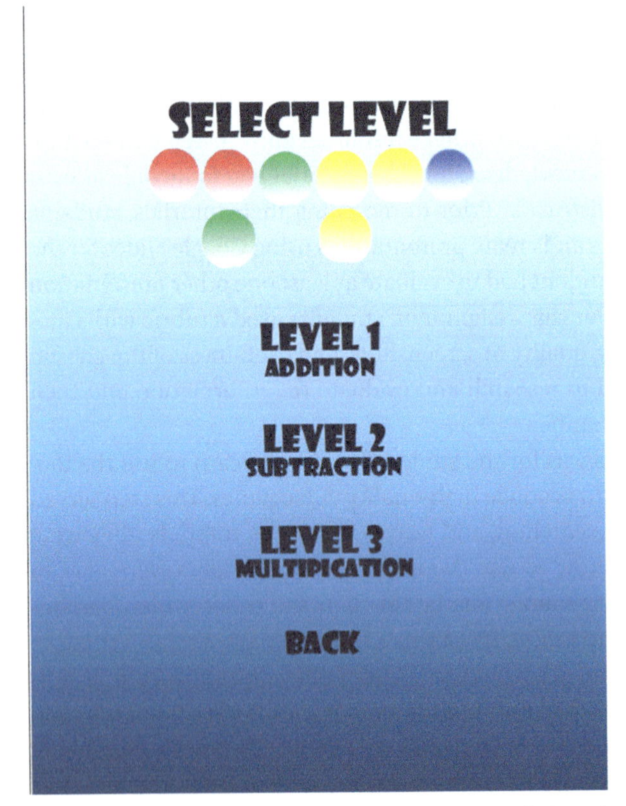

FIGURE 6.3 A screenshot of a student-created game called *Math Blast*

day, which held every student accountable for their individual learning. After creating their first game, they created a video presentation of their games and gameplay. Each student had to explain what the object of their game was and how to win. They evaluated each other's videos. This time, each student

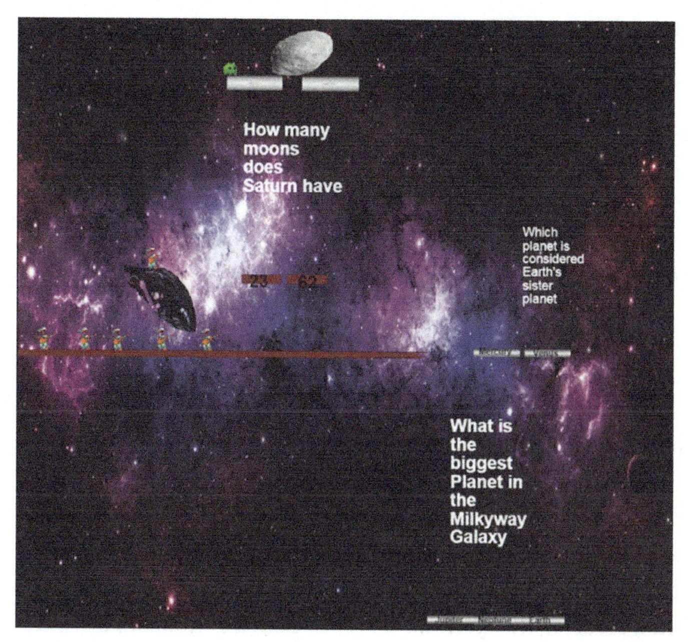

FIGURE 6.4 A screenshot of a student-created game called *Space Explorer*

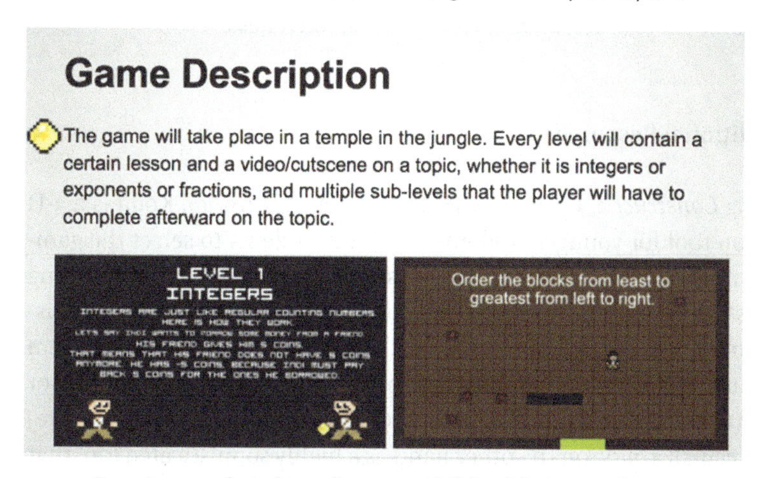

FIGURE 6.5 A screenshot of a student-created slide of their game description

play-tested by playing other students' games and had to provide feedback to the game creator. They were asked to grade if the videogame was playable, if it was useful for learning, and if it was fun enough for high school students. This step allowed the students to gain competency on using the tools.

Finally, students who were interested in the same topic such as history, math, or science created one game in pairs. The pair had to create a working game that was designed to teach specific concepts in a certain subject area.

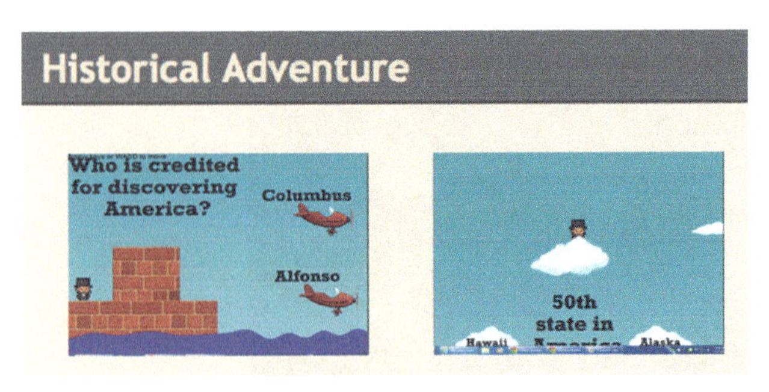

FIGURE 6.6 A screenshot of a student-created slide of their game *Historical Adventure*

Each pair had to submit a planning document that articulated why they chose the subject, particular concepts they wanted to focus on in that subject, and specific game mechanics they were going to use, which demonstrated their critical thinking skills as well as technical knowledge. They also had to discuss the visual aspects of their games. By collaborating with a purpose, students were able to create better products and videos.

After they finished creating the games, everyone spent a couple of days playing all the games. We as a class celebrated which game was the best in terms of aesthetics, game mechanics, and instructional effectiveness.

6 Additional Resources

Prior to using *Construct 2*, I used *Kodu*[2] while teaching *Beowulf*. Kodu is a 3-D game creation tool for younger students. It allows students to select the gaming environment (underwater, dry land, or space), the elevation, and gaming figures. My students used it to create a classic good-against-evil game to illustrate their understanding of the universal theme prevalent in an epic poem *Beowulf*. Many of my colleagues also like to use *Minecraft*,[3] *GameMaker*,[4] or even Unity.[5] *GameMaker* is a tool similar to *Construct 2*, which allows the creation of 2-D games. *Unity*, on the other hand, is a highly sophisticated tool that is typically used by professional game designers. I introduced it to one of my students who is now studying game-development in college.

One additional item to consider is that having the students create analog games can be just as effective.[6]

7 Conclusion

If you are a teacher, you might know how difficult it is for you to stop preparing materials for your students and start letting your students to create. As a former teacher, I remember spending hours creating lecture materials or study guides. I do not believe that teachers should stop doing that. As a matter of fact, direct instruction can be one of the most important instructional methods. However, you can allow your students to learn more about the technological tools by allowing them to participate in the creation process. Furthermore, with the rapid advancement in technological tools, it is important for teachers to leverage the available instructional materials such as YouTube videos. Teachers should also allow students to augment research and evaluation skills. Videogame creation, therefore, can be one of the most targeted and focused ways to target where technological, pedagogical, and content knowledge intersect. By working together on researching and presenting, students can learn more.

8 Connections

8.1 *Things to Remember*

- Teachers need not be the gamer or the game-designer to have this instructional strategy to be successful.
- Having solid rubrics and discussion board – even if they are posters on the wall - is an important component for the success of this lesson. The more transparent and communal the learning experience becomes, the more successful the students will be. This instructional strategy requires a level of collaboration and cooperation. A class culture that encourages students to work together is vital to the success of this strategy.
- Allowing students to explore the use of tools is a valuable instructional strategy. Teachers need not to be the expert user of the technological tools in the classroom. In fact, allowing the students to become the expert can be one of the most powerful learning activities.
- Set realistic instructional objectives for the students. Their job is to learn from the creation process rather than making polished or sophisticated games. Your instruction and assessment should reflect that instructional objective. My additional objective was to teach my students the research and evaluation skills. I also talked a lot about the importance of getting information from credible sources. Finally, I wanted my students to be able to argue for their games even if they were not as aesthetically pleasing.

8.2 *Questions to Ask Yourself If You Are a Teacher*

Q1. What is the purpose of the lesson? Is the lesson meeting the lesson objectives?

Q2. Have I set up the class culture that is conducive to such a highly interactive learning experience? If not, what will I do to encourage that?

Q3. Do I have the minimum technical specifications to make this lesson a success? For example, do I have access to an online discussion format? Do I have a strong Wi-fi connection to sustain the amount of online research being conducted? Do I have access (i.e. licenses) to the game creation tool? If not, what other tools can I use to make this lesson successful?

Q4. Can I gain a similar learning outcome by having them create non-digital games? If so, how would I go about that?

Notes

1 See https://www.scirra.com/construct2
2 See https://www.kodugamelab.com/
3 See https://minecraft.net/en/
4 See http://www.yoyogames.com/gamemaker
5 See https://unity3d.com/
6 For more information on how to do this, you can visit The Kennedy Center's ArtsEdge website: http://artsedge.kennedy-center.org/multimedia/Interactives/artsedge-games/170224-artsedge-games.aspx- ae-games-larp

References

Barab, S., & Squire, K. (2004). Design-based research: Putting a stake in the ground. *Journal of the Learning Sciences, 13*(1), 1–14. doi:10.1207/s15327809jls1301_1

Benkler, Y. (2006). *The wealth of networks*. New Haven, CT: Yale University Press.

Black, R. W. (2008). *Adolescents and online fan fiction*. New York, NY: Peter Lang.

Bogost, I. (2007). *Persuasive games: The expressive power of videogames*. Cambridge, MA: MIT Press.

Bogost, I. (2008). The rhetoric of video games. In K. Salen (Ed.), *The ecology of games: Connecting youth, games, and learning* (pp. 117–140). Cambridge, MA: The MIT Press. doi:10.1162/dmal.9780262693646.117

Brown, J. S., Collins, A., & Duguid, P. (1989). Situated cognition and the culture of learning. *Educational Researcher, 18*(1), 32–42. http://dx.doi.org/10.3102/0013189X018001032

Chai, C. S., Koh, J. H., & Tsai, C. C. (2013). A review of technological pedagogical content knowledge. *Educational Technology & Society, 16*(2), 31–51. Retrieved from http://www.ifets.info/journals/16_2/4.pdf

Chen, M. (2012). *Leet noobs: The life and death of an expert player group in world of warcraft*. New York, NY: Peter Lang Publishing.

Collins, A., Brown, J. S., & Newman, S. E. (1989). Cognitive apprenticeship: Teaching the crafts of reading, writing, and mathematics. In L. B. Resnick (Ed.), *Knowing, learning, and instruction: Essays in honor of Robert Glaser* (pp. 453–494). Hillsdale, NJ: Lawrence Erlbaum Associates.

Construct (Version 2). Computer Software. London: Scirra Ltd.

Gee, J. P. (2003). *What video games have to teach about learning and literacy*. New York, NY: Palgrave MacMillan.

Gee, J. P. (2004). *Situated language and learning: A critique of traditional schooling*. New York, NY: Routledge.

Gee, J. P. (2013). *Good video games + good learning: Collected essays on video games, learning, and literacy* (2nd ed.). New York, NY: Peter Lang.

Greeno, J. (2006). Learning in activity. In K. Sawyer (Ed.), *The Cambridge handbook of the learning sciences* (pp. 79–96). New York, NY: Cambridge University Press.

Jenkins, H. (2006). *Convergence culture: Where old and new media collide* [Kindle DX version]. Retrieved from www.nypress.org

Kafai, Y. B. (2009). Constructionism. In R. K. Sawyer (Ed.), *The Cambridge handbook of learning science* (3rd ed., pp. 35–46). Cambridge: Cambridge University Press.

Koehler, M. J., & Mishra, P. (2009). What is technological pedagogical content knowledge? *Contemporary Issues in Technology and Teacher Education, 9*(1), 60–70.

Koehler, M. J., & Mishra, P. (2012). *The TPACK image* [Online image]. Retrieved February 7, 2017, from tpack.org

Martin, S. L., & Stager, G. (2013). *Invent to learn: Making, tinkering, and engineering in the classroom* [Kindle DX]. Retrieved from www.InventToLearn.com

Mishra, P., & Koehler, M. J. (2006). Technological pedagogical content knowledge: A framework for teacher knowledge. *Teachers College Record, 108*(6), 1017–1054. doi:10.1111/j.1467-9620.2006.00684.x

Papert, S., & Harel, I. (1991). Situating constructionism. In S. Papert & I. Harel (Eds.), *Constructionism*. Ablex Publishing Corporation. Retrieved from http://www.papert.org/articles/SituatingConstructionism.html

Shulman, L. S. (1987). Knowledge and teaching: Foundations of the new reform. *Harvard Educational Review, 57*(1), 1–23. Retrieved from http://people.ucsc.edu/~ktellez/shulman.pdf

Sitzmann, T. (2011). A meta-analytic examination of the instructional effectiveness of computer-based simulation games. *Personnel Psychology, 64*(2), 489–528. doi:10.1111/j.1744-6570.2011.01190.x

Squire, K. (2003). Video games in education. *International Journal of Intelligent*

Games & Simulation, 2(1), 49–62. Retrieved from http://website.education.wisc.edu/~kdsquire/tenure-files/39-squire-IJIS.pdf

Squire, K. (2011). *Video games and learning: Teaching and participatory culture in the digital age*. New York, NY: Teacher College Press.

Van den Akker, J. (2000). Principles and methods of development research. In J. Van den Akker, R. M. Branch, K. Gustafson, N. Nieveen, & T. Plomp (Eds.), *Design approaches and tools in education and training* (pp. 1–14). Dordrecht: Kluwer Academic Publishers.

CHAPTER 7

Practical Advice for Teaching and Learning with Games: Foster Agency and Ownership with an Intentional Approach to Games

Chad Sansing

1 Overarching Questions

1. Do you make intentional efforts to implement gaming in the classroom?
2. What games do you play to grow in your own knowledge of games and gaming integration?
3. Why is it important to know how games are made and designed?
4. How do we become critical consumers and creators of games?

2 Introduction

It takes time and practice to develop a powerful game-based teaching practice. Teaching, like the best games, is a life-long contest against yourself. Where are you now? How do you know? Where do you want to go? How can you get there? How might you make your inevitable failures useful?

When you decide to adopt a games-based teaching practice, you commit yourself to improving as a teacher, gamer, and designer – sometimes by turns and sometimes all at once. You'll make an equal amount of bets, discoveries, and mistakes in an unending attempt to make your learners feel like participants in – and owners of – their education.

That doesn't mean you have to be teacher of the year, speed-run every game you play, or compose flawless lesson plans day after day. Instead, it means that you intentionally habituate yourself to understanding what games can and can't do for you and your learners. Over time, your understanding will broaden and deepen – in the same way you see teaching and learning everywhere, you'll begin to see games everywhere, and then you'll begin to see the decisions that make up each teaching, learning, and gaming opportunity, similar to the way a designer sees the parts of the parts of the whole.

Take your strengths as a teacher, learner, gamer, or designer and use them to power your growth in other areas of games-based teaching and learning. If

 | DOI: 10.1163/9789004422315_010

you have a strong handle on curriculum development, apply the processes you use to analyzing and composing games for your students. Play lots of games yourself to see how they're similar to and different from the work you produce.

If you have a lot of experience as a gamer, tap into the ways games teach players through feedback and play loops. You might also take the emotional truths of what makes a game feel good and build lesson plans that might help your learners connect to the same feelings in a more explicitly educational context.

If the design process suits you best, look at how games and teacher-mentors relate to their learners, players, or users. Repeatedly test and iterate your work until it makes sense to the people you design for – your students.

This is all general advice meant to encourage you to consider gaming as another form of teaching and learning – one you can train yourself to look for and use in your classroom whether it's a formal or informal one. What follows are more practical pieces of advice for implementing the game-based ideas you develop as a teacher, gamers, and designer. Not every piece of advice will be for you; in many cases, you will already know better. However, by considering the pragmatic suggestions below as a whole, you might see a bigger picture than you did before, or you might visit part of a bigger picture you haven't paid much attention to in the past. In either case: onward.

3 Play a Lot of Games

The best way to become a better games-based teacher is to play a lot of games.

This seems obvious, but it doesn't feel that way. The best games involve us in stories we co-create as players. We make decisions; those decisions have consequences we experience in-game (and sometimes in our lives). We have fun – either on our own or in community. We talk back to the games. These are all behaviors that traditional schooling discourages.

School expects us to produce results, not to make decisions. It tends to deliver the same kind of work and experience routinely despite the choices we make on any given school day. It is, to a stifling extent, student and teacher-agnostic. School expects us to be alone in a crowd – to travel with dozens of peers from place to place, but to interact mostly (and mostly obediently) with a single adult in each classroom. It doesn't account for our emotional states or well-being; we might be laughing; we might be crying; either way, we're disrupting "the work" and typically sent out to hide our sadness, happiness, incredulity, or anger from everyone else.

However, games want us to feel something and very often they want us to feel something in community.

Playing a lot of games helps you

- Discover and understand how to use different genres, mechanics, and narratives in your classroom.
- Understand and plan for the emotional outcomes of different kinds of games in your classroom.
- Design games and game-design projects for students that maximize individual and collective engagement with delightful, relevant work.

Read about games – board games, card games, party games, role playing games, video games, and any other kinds of games you can find. Find out what's popular and why those games work better than others. Find their online communities and message boards. Think about researching and learning these games the same way you think about reading blog posts from your favorite teachers and new books about assessment and teaching strategies from your favorite educational authors.

Make playing games part of your professional practice. Make and protect time for it. Maybe start a games-based reading group at school with your professional learning community (PLC) or critical friends. You could spend each marking period or semester on a game or genre and help each other create and test lesson plans using the games you play or mechanics you borrow from them. This kind of professional development practice gives you and your peers a community in which you can support and challenge each other to take risks in your own learning and reflect on them.

Each of you might find a particular game or genre you love and become expert at it – a go-to resource for the group.

Playing games together will also help you understand what success and failure feel like in those games. This will let you better plan for unwinding and reflection after playing games in class. For example, you might help one another think of what kinds of scaffolds and questions you craft for the "losers" so their voices remain powerful and insightful while discussing the games they lost as opportunities to learn from their mistakes or from decisions made by the "winners". If you know one game feels low-stakes and silly while another feels engrossing and intense, you can chunk playtime or plan for emotional check-ins accordingly to make sure your students are all okay throughout a game.

Even if you can't form a gaming group with colleagues from your PLC, you should play games with your friends and concentrate on learning how each game works and feels. Ask your friends how they would feel if they won or lost in a classroom setting. Ask them what they think a game teaches its players.

Pay attention to their responses – and to your own – as players. If you're going to use games in your classroom, you have to be prepared to help students process the emotional truths they feel as they play. Games are not worksheets or poster or slide decks. Even having fun is an emotional investment that can be risky to make in a formal educational setting. You need to be a "game master" who can explain and clarify the rules of the games your students play, but you also need to be a caring adult who prepares players for the emotions they might feel during play and assures them that those feelings are a normal, safe, and valid part of your classroom and community.

3.1 *Types of Games*

Note: many games and platforms can be adapted to work as several different kinds of games.

- Single-player: games in which a single player plays against the rules and the game itself like a Choose Your Own Adventure (CYOA) book, Sudoku, or solitaire.
- Multiplayer competitive: games in which individual players work against one another like chess, Monopoly, or tic-tac-toe.
- Multiplayer social collaborative: games in which players or teams of players work together to win like *Dungeons & Dragons*, *Pandemic*, or *A Slow Year.*
- Multiplayer social competitive: games in which asymmetric or symmetric teams of players work against one another like charades, football, or Werewolf.

4 Understand How Games Work

Games are manipulative – they encourage us to suspend our disbelief, to immerse ourselves in the decision-making of each game, and to feel the emotions the game is meant to deliver on cure in response to different events in the game and decisions made by its players. The best games match mechanics and rules with narratives that reinforce one another so that as you get better at the game, you feel like you impact the game and other players more than the rules impact you.

Games typically use real-time feedback to spur learning. When you play a well-designed game, you know how well you're doing almost all the time and you're presented with choices that are governed by rules, mechanics, and narrative. Rule books, tutorials, experienced players, and house rules like "take backs" help you pick the best decisions early on, but as you become more skilled you tend to make your own decisions and accept their consequences as a way of matching the game's difficulty to your level of play. Making the right decision on your own later on delivers a similar kind of emotional fulfillment of discovering the right decision early on with help from others. That feeling of success combines with the story of the game to make you feel immersed in it as an agent and owner of your own experience.

Think of your favorite games for a few minutes. During gameplay or over time, wow do they use features like these to keep you playing?

- Real-time feedback.
- Decision-making loops.
- Scaling difficulty.
- Story.

How do you use features like these in the curriculum you use or produce? How immediately do your learners get feedback directly related to their performance with class content? How often do they get to make their own decisions about what to learn and how to learn it? How well do your materials scale with difficulty to support novices and challenge experts? What is the story arc of your classroom? Of your academic year? Is it clear to students? Do they feel a part of it? What connects each daily episode to a larger narrative of engagement, progress, or success?

Not every day in games-based classroom is a resounding success in every area of game design and play. However, if you want to teach and learn in a games-based classroom, you have to work intentionally over time to design with these features in mind.

5 Understand How You Might Use Games in Your Classroom

When you make the decision to work towards a game-based classroom, you commit yourself to using game-design principles and features to design curriculum that gives learners agency and ownership over their work and the story of the learning. Working within those guidelines, you can run a games-based classroom that doesn't seem to use many games. Maybe it seems like a connected or democratic classroom, a participatory one, or one run according to student inquiry. The best classrooms, like the best games, deliver on real-time feedback, student decision-making, scaling difficulty and support, and a compelling story of self for each student that helps them each understand their learning and growth as an individual accomplishment supported by a caring community of teachers and peers.

Conversely, you can use games all the time and still not have a games-based classroom. You can offer games during "free time" or as an "extension" for students who successfully complete the work you assign before your peers. You can use games episodically and without much reflection when they have a thematic connection to your core content. You can use games that are essentially rote, closed systems to teach a single concept, skill, or piece of vocabulary again and again.

You cross over the border from using games to running a game-based classroom when you decide to design your curriculum according to your students' needs for feedback, agency, growth, connection-making, and relevancy. Your deliberate use of games becomes clear and informative to them. They understand what they're supposed to learn and how they're supposed to learn from the games, as well. You create a culture of safe, constructive, and timely feedback in response to the decisions students make about their learning, the challenges they take on, and the way they frame success and failure as invitations or obstacles to moving ahead in class.

You might ask students to play a game you bought at the store or downloaded from an online shop. You might share a game you designed on your own. You might launch a student game-design project. What matters most is that you treat your students like people, learners, and game players who want to improve instead of treating them like employees, workers, or a captive audience. Design for them instead of demanding that they work for you.

That takes a lot of work – work that lasts for years and involves countless failures and, often, invisible success. That is our game – the system in which we get to make decisions that we think will help students and in which they give us pretty immediate feedback about how well we meet and fail the challenges we've chosen for ourselves as part of our life's work. Failure, losing, and the naked impossibility of reaching every student every day are invitations to try again, rather than discouragements from it. There is no obstacle to making the attempt apart from us. We stand in our own way, or we don't. We learn to get out of our own way, to sidestep the shadows we cast at ourselves from places of institutional fear. We quest.

6 Make Games Accessible and Inviting

Practice #mimi: make it more inviting. Consider your students as you adapt, adopt, and design games for them. Use games that speak to your learners, rather than to yourself. Be ready to explain and demo for students who struggle with blocks of rules text. Be ready to provide alternative text that describes game boards, pieces, graphic, and illustrations for students who struggle to see them. Have alternative sets of core gameplay mechanics for students who struggle to move or manipulate objects one way or another. Use games that represent all of your students positively. Use games that matter to your students.

It doesn't do any good to use or create the perfect game for half your students. It fractures your classroom community and creates feelings of unfairness and injustice when something you present as valuable doesn't value all of your students. Approaching game-based learning carelessly is a lot like approaching group work carelessly. Someone will wind up "playing all the game" and resenting you and the other players while the other players resent you and the "winner" because no one made it clear to them how or why to play the game.

You might plan for students to team up with one another to make decisions even if one partner mostly reads the game's text or moves it pieces. You might move all the pieces in a game in response to instructions from your students. Your game may not have pieces or text at all. You may challenge students to find as many ways to play a game as possible.

There's no set expectation of how you can adapt or design a game – or to create a menu of games – to be inviting to everyone. Think of what you want every student to learn; think of how each learns best; use or adapt a game or set or games that provides balanced, inviting access to that learning. Talk about different ways students can play before you begin. Ask how a competitive game might be made collaborative, instead. Acknowledge problem areas of accessibility, equity, and inclusion. Invite more just remixes and new styles of play. Involve students in making decisions about how they'll play in pursuit of what you want them to learn.

Demonstrate your willingness to change the rules to advantage your students and their learning and invite them to do the same. That's the kind of critical thinking, decision-making, and working in community that will make games-based learning a force for good in your classroom.

You can use something like a game jam to habituate yourself and your students to looking at games this way.

1. Plan to take a few days of class time for the game jam.
2. Gather a collection of different games and craft supplies.
3. Take apart all the games and bag their pieces like dice, meeples (the little "people" you move around a gameboard), and play money.
4. Put all the separated parts of those games and all the craft supplies on a table.
5. Form equitable groups of students.
6. Invite one student to be the "curator" and to select a bunch of materials to bring back to the group.
7. Let the curator set up those materials and then take a seat as the last person to take a turn in the game.

8. Figure out who goes first in each group, knowing the curator will go last.
9. Then the player who goes first makes up 1 rule and takes 1 move in the game; someone in the group records that rule.
10. Each subsequent player can change or get rid of 1 rule or make 1 new rule.
11. The game continues until each group has made a game that's fun for all the players.
12. After the game jam, each explains how they created a game that was fun for everyone and shares their rules with the whole group.

This is a collaborative, participatory design experiment that works because learners change, remix, and, in some cases, ignore the "rules" in favor of designing something that works for the group. This is also a great professional development (PD) activity for colleagues who seem skeptical about games-based learning.

After players see what's possible, you can ask them what it would take to make your classroom feel the way they felt while playing. Their answers can become design principles that complement universal feature of game-based practice like real-time feedback and scaling difficulty.

7 Be Critical of the Games You Play and the Decisions You Make to Use Them

A quick note on using games in the classroom: don't bring harmful games into your community.

Pay attention to the games you use and design in the same way to preview texts, videos, and speakers. For example, there are many popular games and genres that encourage trash talk, glorify violence, and sexualize characters. While your learners might play some of these games outside your community and while your learners may have experienced and fought against verbal abuse, violence, or sexual harassment, that doesn't mean those topics are fair game at all times for a safe, supportive classroom community, even as objects to analyze and critique.

If you think a game has a good mechanic for learning or a compelling story, but it's potentially harmful to learners in your classroom, don't be its ambassador. Find an alternative or design something that captures the idea of the mechanic or the flow of the story without communicating its content to your students. Game-based learning is not a call to seem "edgy". "hip", or "young" to your students. Let them trust you to provide consistently constructive examples of games and analysis that they can use to explore their own lives and learning. Don't ever try to shock them into game-based learning. That is not the "withitness" they need from you.

A student may ask you if they can do some work with a game you would never bring to class. You should negotiate that request with the student, their parents, and your administration. However, you should not teach with a gaming "text" that has the potential to harm people in your care. Trust yourself, your students, and support staff to find appropriate and constructive ways to tackle important subjects like equity, justice, and trolling through games that don't alienate, harm, or victimize your students.

You're not a bad person just for playing a game at home that you would never bring to class (though you should examine what your own gaming behavior says about your prejudices), but don't err on the side of arrogance and think you can facilitate a constructive discussion off the cuff about a game celebrating destructive behavior.

It's much better to ask your students something like, "What advice do you have for game designers who only seem include stereotypical characters in their games?", than to do something like demo a game full of stereotypes and ask students to document them all.

At the same time, if you wind up introducing a game that you think is exemplary and a student calls out a prejudice in it, acknowledge that call out, see if you can facilitate a discussion about its presence in the game and impact on it, and make a decision with your learners to try something else, as warranted. Don't shy away from student criticism of the games you use and create in class; don't shy away from discussing important societal issues surfaced in games.

Have those crucial conversations, but do so in a way that values your students' safety and empowers them to identify and pose solutions to the problems they see.

8 Reflection, Reflection, Reflection

Playing games is only part of the work of a games-based classroom. To capture student learning, you need to foster a reflective community, as well.

Be sure to provide time for reflection before, during, and after gameplay. For example, before play, you might ask questions like these:

- What do you think this game will be about?
- What kinds of decisions do you think you'll have to make?
- What strategies do you predict might be successful in this game?

During play you can ask learners to keep a log that records their decisions and reasoning after each round.

After the game, you can ask students to critique the game and their play using questions like these:

- In your own words, what did you learn from the game? Think about what you learned about the game, but also about what you learned for class.
- Were your predictions about the game mostly correct or incorrect? What surprised you?
- What mechanics, rules, or story elements made this game good or bad for you as a player?
- Would you play this game again? Why or why not?
- How would you play differently next time?
- Are there any parts of this game you would borrow and use in your own game designs? Which ones? Why?

Answering questions like these gives students the chance to evaluate their own decisions, as well as the qualities of the games they play and learn from in class. They can develop this reflective practice to help them better design their own games later on and they can use these questions to critique one another's games in a constructive, predictable, and routine way.

The key to showing students how they learn from games is to get them to reflect, in their own words, on their own experiences.

Be sure to provide enough different ways to reflect that no student feels limited by the format or technology you use. You might provide a worksheet, as well as a shared document, as well as a piece of recording software, as well as an opportunity to dictate answers to a peer or adult who can type them for a student. Giving every student the choice of how to reflect is absolutely in line with the key features of game-based learning like providing real-time feedback (for you and them!) decision-making, scaling difficulty, and co-creating story.

9 Game Design and Group Work

After you and your learners have a significant amount of shared experience with game-based learning, you can use game-design as a way to fuel inquiry and more traditional content mastery.

You can design increasingly open games about learning itself or more limited, but compelling closed or "single use" games about particular pieces of content addressed in your curriculum.

Likewise, students can use game design principles to drive their own inquiry-based learning about content or to demonstrate mastery of content you assign or teach.

Some students might be ready to design games on their own. Others might prefer group work. If you decide to use group work as a support for game design projects, be sure to demo and coach students on different roles they can play.

For example, one student might be a project-manager, keeping track of peers' work, pitching in as needed, and reporting on group progress to you. Another might work on prototyping game pieces while a third drafts the games' rules. While it's probably best for group members to brainstorm individually and then together to review their ideas for games and pick an idea to pursue by consensus, you don't want a group with three project managers or concept artists with no one working on rules.

Be intentional in how you structure and support groups. You might even need to have a meeting every day with every like-jobbed student across groups when you begin just so everyone understands their role. For example, you could meet with all of a class's project managers to coach them on giving feedback and then meet with all of the game artists to share online illustration tools and then meet with all of the writers to decide on a consistent format for drafting each group's rules.

Likewise, be intentional about the design process you ask students to follow, support them with shared documents and coaching on how to approach, research, brainstorm, prototype, and test in response to a game design problem. For example, you might lead them through steps like these over several chunks of time or class periods:

1. *Identify the problem:* What does their game need to demonstrate or teach? What problem does it present or solve for its players? You might present this problem to students or they might suggest their own ("We need a game that teaches everyone in the cafeterias to recycle").
2. *Research the problem:* What other games have similar mechanics or stories? How do they work? What makes them successful? How could they be improved? What does the game's audience need from it?
3. *Brainstorm possible solutions:* Have each group member come up with ideas to share; given them a good amount of time to generate their own ideas before they share with their groups.
4. *Evaluate those solutions:* Which idea – or combination of ideas – for a game seems best to the whole group? Which idea or combinations seems most likely to solve the design problem?
5. *Prototype the solution:* This is when students should take on different roles and tackle different parts of the project.
6. *Test the solution:* This is when students should play other groups' games and give feedback on them.
7. *Iterate the solution:* When you iterate on a solution, you improve it in response to feedback. Groups can test and iterate several times.

8. *Share your solution:* This is when students present their "finished" games to you, one another, and/or community stakeholders.

By using a design process like this over and over to scaffold students' game design work, you help them develop analytical habits they can use for self-assessment and growth. You help them see design and reflection as extensions of one another and you help them value their peers and communities as audiences and trusted critics of their work.

10 Encourage Ownership and Innovation

When in doubt, err on the side of student ownership, inquiry, and innovation. Over time you'll find a core set of games you like to use to teach particular concepts and mechanics. Mark those game boxes and inventory them. Share their significance with your learners and make them available to play outside of your lessons, as well. It's a good idea to have a library of exemplary games you and your students can reference in discussion through your time together.

However, in a game-based classroom, students should feel like they have ownership over not only their learning, but the tools they use to learn. There is no law that says you have to keep everything that comes in a new game box just so. There are no rules – just norms – that prevent us from mixing and matching games and game pieces however we want.

If you want to move toward game-design as a form on inquiry or production in your classroom, you should have a games toolbox in addition to a games library. Keep those pieces you separated out for your game jam handy in a centralized, easily accessible location. Make prototyping games as "easy" as brainstorming or pre-writing. Make it possible to have a games lab or playground in your classroom whenever you need to demo something or whenever students need materials in front of them to puzzle out a mechanic.

Let students bring a meeple to class, even when you invite them to pay attention to you for a lesson or meeting. Let them own their behavior, as well as those game pieces. See if they settle and can satisfy other sensory needs with game pieces or game design tools while you share your ideas with the group. Maybe having materials nearby and under their control will help them concretize and better understand – or improve on – what you have to say.

Don't build a games-based classroom where games and their pieces are off limits except when you say so. It's probably not a great idea to have different groups of students playing different games while you try to teach a new mechanic for the first time, but having students work through your demo with authentic materials lets them own the means of production in your room (for the semester or year, at least) and can be trusted to learn and invent in a workshop environment that values their agency and contribution of attention to the lessons you teach there.

11 Bend the Arc of Your Games-Based Practices towards Social Justice

Finally, for now, ask yourself why you and your students should game. What makes a great game such an effective piece of media for communicating ideas and feelings? What do people do with those ideas and feelings in real life after they finish or master a game? What can they transfer from that experience to a problem the face elsewhere in their experiences?

Help your students understand gaming as a way to learn design and to prototype their responses to the world around them. Encourage them to create games that address the inequities and injustices they see in the world. Help them teach others how to help themselves and their communities through games. Connect them with a network of audiences and stakeholders outside the classroom. Find mentors in game development and activities in communities and officials in government who can take what they've made, help them improve it, and put it in front communities facing the same problems your students face.

Games can be a pastime and escape. Sometimes, we need those things. There are things in life to escape from.

However, they also carry empowering stories in their narratives and construction. They can teach agency, analysis, critique, design, ownership, problem-solving, and community-building.

Those are the outcomes you should pursue for your students; game-based learning gives you one way to work towards a more equitable, just future shaped by students who understand the rules of the game and, most importantly, that they can change them.

Index

Printed in the United States
By Bookmasters